Jan 2017

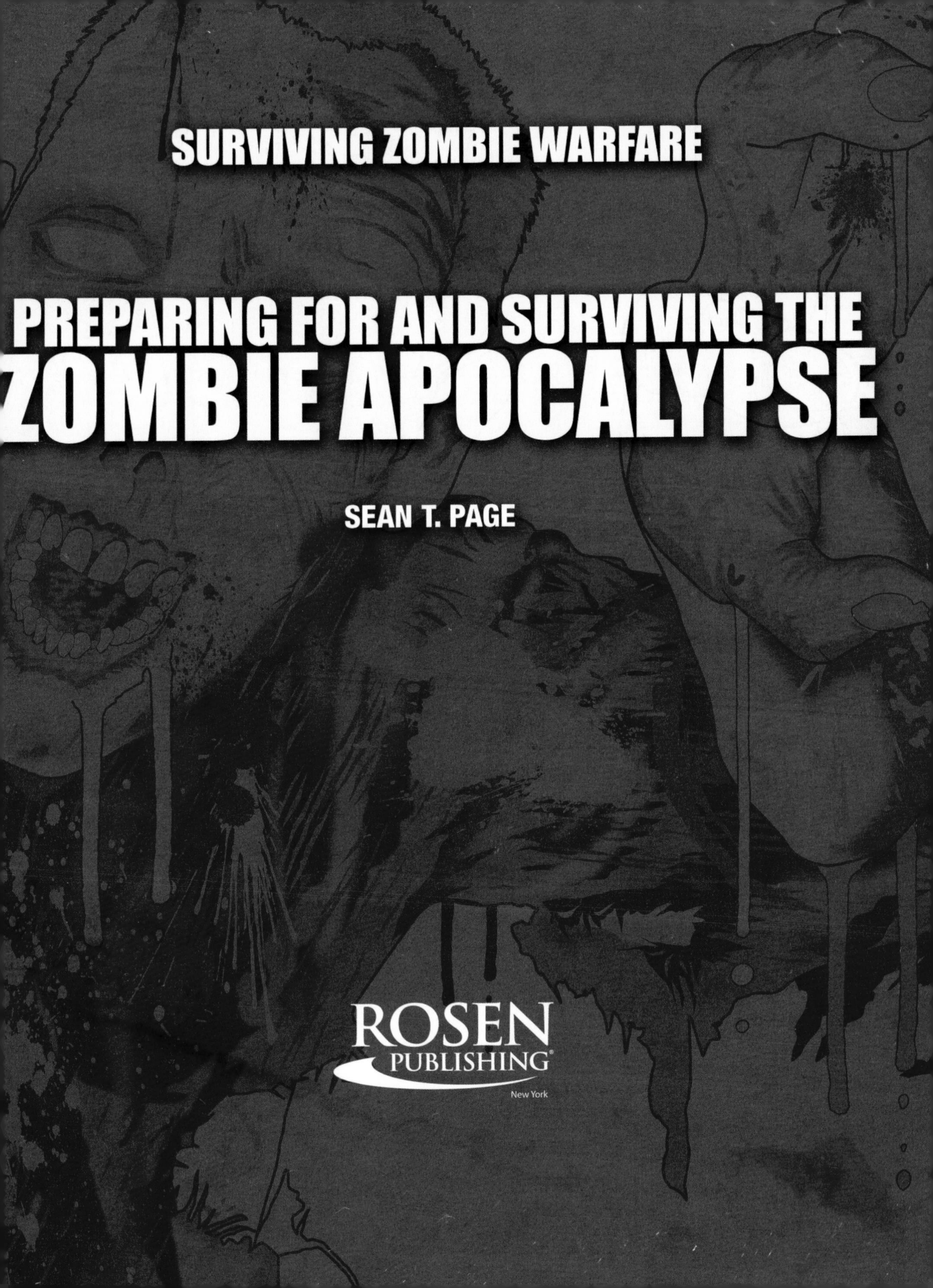

SURVIVING ZOMBIE WARFARE

PREPARING FOR AND SURVIVING THE
ZOMBIE APOCALYPSE

SEAN T. PAGE

ROSEN
PUBLISHING®

New York

This edition published in 2017 by:

The Rosen Publishing Group, Inc.
29 East 21st Street
New York, NY 10010

Library of Congress Cataloging-in-Publication Date t/k

Names: Page, Sean T.
Title: Preparing for and surviving the zombie apocalypse / Sean T. Page.
Other titles: Zombie survival manual
Description: New York : Rosen Publishing, 2017. | Series: Surviving zombie warfare | "Originally published by Haynes Publishing under the title: Zombie survival manual." | Includes bibliographical references and index.
Identifiers: LCCN 2016002167
ISBN 9781499463866 (library bound)
ISBN 9781499463842 (pbk.)
ISBN 9781499463859 (6-pack)
Subjects: LCSH: Zombies--Humor.
Classification: LCC PN6231.Z65 P36 2016 | DDC 818/.602--dc23
LC record available at http://lccn.loc.gov/2016002167

Manufactured in the United States of America

Originally published in English by Haynes Publishing under the title: Zombie Survival Manual © Sean T. Page 2013.

MINISTRY OF ZOMBIES

CONTENTS

HOME PREPARATION AND DEFENSE

It is not uncommon for readers taking zombies seriously for the first time to have that 'light bulb' moment when they realize that the walking dead are a real threat to our way of life and that without some serious preparation, things are going to get ugly very quickly.

Before even looking at your own zombie preparation plans, it is important to understand the key principles of home defense against the dead.

It is important to grasp how remorseless these creatures are. They may not win any prizes in general intelligence, but they will claw, scratch and push their way into the homes of many of the unprepared. It shocks many new to zombie survival to discover that one of the safest places to be during a zombie apocalypse is actually in the comfort of your own home. Imagine the chaos out on the streets as the dead mix freely with the living and confusion abounds? Wouldn't you rather be tucked up safely in your own zombie-proof home? The following pages will provide you with knowledge and skills not only to stay safe in the home but also to survive for more than 90 days in a home cut off from the world.

ZOMBIE PROOFING DIY

It is not uncommon for trainee zombie survivalists to start looking around their home and quickly become overwhelmed by the sheer number of jobs which require attention. For example, should we have built a six-foot (1.8-m) brick wall instead of that rock garden or would the money paid for laying a new lawn have been better spent on setting punji stake pits along the drive? However, do not panic! The Ministry of Zombies has created a complete home audit system which you can use to assess your home in its current condition and develop a realistic plan to start addressing the key areas of zombie defense weakness. Remember, not everything needs to be done at once, and many of the improvements are low cost.

However, before completing a home audit you should learn the basics of zombie home defense. This simple model was laid down in the 1990s and is known in the wider zombie-fighting community as the 'Principles of Zombie Home Defense'. In a nutshell, these principles recommend three lines of defense against the dead for any dwelling.

HOME PREPARATION AND DEFENSE
SAFEST PLACES TO BE DURING A ZOMBIE APOCALYPSE

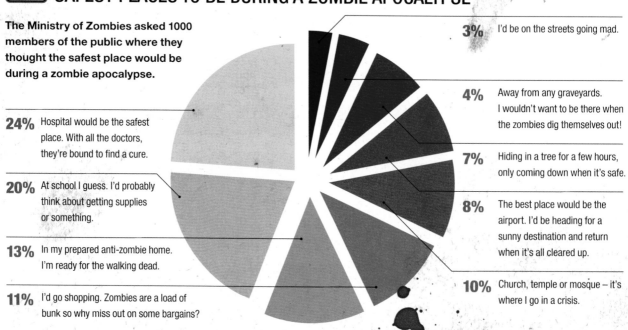

The Ministry of Zombies asked 1000 members of the public where they thought the safest place would be during a zombie apocalypse.

24% Hospital would be the safest place. With all the doctors, they're bound to find a cure.

20% At school I guess. I'd probably think about getting supplies or something.

13% In my prepared anti-zombie home. I'm ready for the walking dead.

11% I'd go shopping. Zombies are a load of bunk so why miss out on some bargains?

3% I'd be on the streets going mad.

4% Away from any graveyards. I wouldn't want to be there when the zombies dig themselves out!

7% Hiding in a tree for a few hours, only coming down when it's safe.

8% The best place would be the airport. I'd be heading for a sunny destination and return when it's all cleared up.

10% Church, temple or mosque – it's where I go in a crisis.

SURVEY VERIFIED BY THE MARKET INSIGHT GROUP

> PRINCIPLES OF ZOMBIE HOME DEFENSE

1ST PRINCIPLE
EXTERNAL PERIMETER

The first principle of any defense against the dead is to have a robust external perimeter. In most cases, this will be a garden fence or wall, but equally the same principles would apply if you were defending a shop, a police station or any building. The external perimeter is your first line of defense and if breached should enable you to fall back in good order.

2ND PRINCIPLE
INTERIOR PERIMETER

The second principle of defense against the dead is to have a 'zombie proof' interior perimeter. In reality, no location or defensive line can ever be 100% zombie proof – the dead will always find a way in eventually. However, in a typical residential scenario this interior perimeter should include double-glazed or barred windows and strong doors. If the horde breaks through your first line, you should be able to slam that front door and be safe from the zombies as you regroup. Within your interior perimeter is the so-called 'green zone' where any living quarters will be. Survivors can normally move around this area unarmed.

EXTERNAL PERIMETER
GARDEN FENCE OR WALL

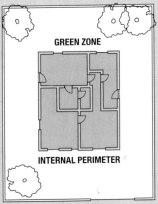

GREEN ZONE

INTERNAL PERIMETER

EXTERNAL PERIMETER

INTERNAL PERIMETER
WALLS, WINDOWS AND DOORS

SAFE ROOM

INTERNAL PERIMETER

SAFE ROOM
FALL-BACK POSITION

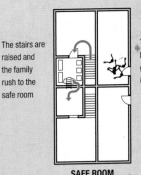

The stairs are raised and the family rush to the safe room

The zombies burst in and ground floor is overrun

SAFE ROOM

3RD PRINCIPLE
FINAL LINE OF DEFENSE

The third principle of zombie defense is the creation of a final line of defense or a 'safe room'. This is your ultimate fallback position if your home is overrun. In this scenario, survivors typically have very little time to plan, perhaps the dead have forced a door open or someone has accidentally let them through a window. Whatever the cause, the impact is akin to a tidal wave of rotting ghouls flooding into the house. You and your group therefore need a location which is secure, to re-group again and plan your next move. The safe room does not actually need to be a room – many survivors remove ground-floor stairs so they can cut off their upper floors if required. Any safe room must have basic supplies, strong doors and any essentials you feel necessary for a break out. Many survivors create escape routes through the ceiling of safe rooms – possibly moving into the next house through the loft. In the early days of the apocalypse, you and your group may sleep sealed in the safe room for extra security, but do not forget you should always have a guard on duty.

⚠ WARNING

UNLIKE MANY OF THE PRE-BUILT COMMERCIALLY AVAILABLE SAFE ROOMS ON THE MARKET TODAY, A ZOMBIE SAFE ROOM IS NOT A LOCATION TO LOCK YOURSELF IN UNTIL HELP ARRIVES. IF YOU LOCK YOURSELF IN A REGULAR SAFE ROOM AS THE DEAD PILE UP AGAINST THE DOOR, IT COULD BECOME YOUR TOMB AS YOU WILL BE UNABLE TO ESCAPE AND THIS TIME, HELP CERTAINLY WON'T BE COMING! A ZOMBIE SAFE ROOM MUST ALWAYS HAVE AN ALTERNATIVE EXIT...

HOME PREPARATION AND DEFENSE

THE ZOMBIE HOME PREPARATION AUDIT

The home survey opposite was developed in conjunction with the Home Builders Association of America, the British Building Standards Group and the Irish Institute of Construction. You should print a copy and try to approach your home with 'fresh eyes'. It is important to get inside the mind of a zombie and imagine their attack points. Try wearing a yellow safety hat and use a clip board when you are completing the work to give you that 'official' look.

Walk methodically around your home 'scoring' against the various criteria on the form. If necessary, hire an expert to complete the survey. A completed Zombie Home Preparation Audit is the place to start in zombie home defense, regardless of the score.

HOW IT WORKS

Each home or location starts with 100 points and points are deducted for each risk assessed. You can improve your home score over time by mitigating a risk. We have included some examples, but feel free to deduct more points for any other extra hazards. Be harsh with your scoring.

Complete the form, but do not be alarmed if the results are poor at first. If you score zero in some categories you may wish to move on. For example, if you are next to a hospital or in an unsuitable rented property then consider moving immediately.

On completing this assessment, your first action should be to prioritize a list of measures to improve any future assessment. Remember that you should not start spending serious money on bulking items such as underground water storage tanks while forgetting about areas such as double-glazing and essential roof repairs. Get the basics right first then develop your property.

Final note on home defense: it's not all about the zombies. With the zombie apocalypse will come armies of looters and unmentionables. So, if you are sitting in a superb zombie fortification that everyone knows about, be prepared for them paying you a visit. It may be worth making any improvements in secret and even giving your home that 'worn out' look to fool any would-be human attackers.

They say there's 'no place like home' and if you get your preparation right, you will have made a major step towards surviving the zombies so approach the whole audit process seriously and with the knowledge that detailed and critical observation now could prevent one of your loved ones becoming a snack for the ghouls.

ANALYZING THE RESULTS

Originally, the Zombie Home Preparation Audit was meant to be completed by trained professionals to form part of a Home Information Pack whenever a residence is sold or let, but changes in government policy in both the USA and UK have meant that you now need to complete this work yourself. The information below offers some general advice based on your score. Remember, these are generic guidelines as every home is different.

If one 'area of investigation' scores zero and there is no practical way to mitigate the risk then consider moving as soon as possible. For example, you may live next door to a high-risk site or a prime looting location, in which case, it's time to start packing.

LESS THAN 40

You and your family are in serious danger of being a cheap meat snack the moment the dead arrive. There are just too many holes in your zombie defenses. If you can't improve the situation, move.

40 TO 60

A reasonable score for a first assessment but where you have identified areas of improvement, make those changes now.

61 TO 80

A great start. Either you have made some improvements already or you have bought or rented a property very wisely. Build on your current defenses and keep it up. You have a good chance of surviving the initial chaos so keep going and always look for ways to take things to the next level. For example, could you convert that rock garden into an M-60 machine gun pit? It's just a suggestion.

81 TO 100

You've given yourself a real chance of survival, but are there any small improvements you could make? Equally, always be careful that your home is not too obvious in its defenses. If you run around the neighborhood boasting of the zombie robustness of your home – guess where everyone is going to head for when the chaos starts? Any secure home fortress that is too obvious will be an invitation to every desperate survivor out there who won't think twice about scooting in there while you are in the yard and locking you out.

AREA OF INVESTIGATION	HAZARDS TO BE ASSESSED	SCORE
Exterior Hazards and Environs The site location and surrounding area	▶ Close to hospital, place of worship etc. ▶ Close proximity to 'looting' location. ▶ No access to clean water source. ▶ Telephone pole or tree nearby.	/10
Property Visual Inspection How well maintained the property is in general	▶ Poorly maintained building. ▶ Only one access point. ▶ No chimney or open fire. ▶ Poorly maintained roof/broken tiles.	/10
Outer Perimeter The robustness of the external perimeter such as the property boundary or exterior fencing	▶ No secure outside yard. ▶ No secure outside buildings. ▶ Inadequate exterior fencing.	/20
Inner Perimeter The robustness of the internal perimeter such as windows, doors and any other access points	▶ No double-glazing. ▶ Poorly fitted doors or rotting frames. ▶ Small, unbarred low windows.	/20
Safe Room Potential Assessing the property's capabilities if zombies break in	▶ Single storey. ▶ Weak interior doors. ▶ Poor internal layout with too many 'dead ends'.	/10
Self-sufficiency Potential Comfort and resources over the medium to long term	▶ Poor storage potential. ▶ No secure basement. ▶ No secure outside space. ▶ Limited water storage.	/20
Zombie Attack Role Play A freestyle role play attack, highlighting any weak points	▶ Zombies' ability to gain access. ▶ Zombies collapsing an exterior fence. ▶ Zombies forcing open a garage door. ▶ Zombies managing to reach through poorly secured window.	/10

TOTAL SCORE OUT OF 100

HOME PREPARATION AND DEFENSE

TOP HOME REPAIR TIPS

Defending against the zombies starts with the basics. It's pointless spending a fortune on the ultimate zombie safe room if your home is poorly insulated, the roof is in danger of collapsing or the front door is coming off its hinges.

Looking at all the areas that require attention can easily overwhelm the new zombie survivalist so the Ministry of Zombies has created a simple six-step process to creating a safer home. It may surprise people to find that steps such as gaining invaluable DIY skills and insulating your home come before smashing up the stairs. Use a completed zombie home preparation audit along with these six key pointers to get yourself and your house ready for a major zombie outbreak and remember, not everything will be about buying more planks of wood.

1 YOUR OWN DIY SKILLS

Every zombie survivalist should also be a do-it-yourself expert. You won't be able to call a plumber during the zombie apocalypse so learn the basics now. The same goes for carpentry and basic building work. Get on as many courses as you can and ensure you have the right tools. The better you know your household, the more you will be able to rely on your skills to defend it when you have to.

2 WALL AND LOFT INSULATION

It makes sense to ensure that your home is as insulated as possible to protect you and your family in the cold months ahead. So, this includes wall and attic insulation. The zombie survivalist should also explore solar panels, wind generators and reliable diesel generators for when the power goes down. Get an Energy Performance Certificate commissioned if you are unsure of what to do.

3 WINDOWS AND DOORS

Double glazing is a cost-effective improvement to any home but will pay dividends once the electricity goes off and you are left with little heating. In addition, zombies cannot break through such windows. Consider triple-glazing if you can and then the option of adding bars or a steel rolling blind. Pay particular attention to door frames as they are often overlooked – it is pointless having a strong door only to have it cave in under the pressure of the zombies due to a poorly fitted frame!

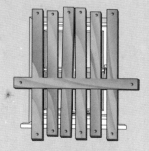

1 Hammer planks over the windows then place a support across. 40% of all zombie break-ins are through open windows – so back them!

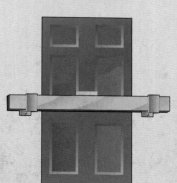

2 A basic support will strengthen any door. It only works on doors that open inwards.

A wedged bar at the bottom of the stairs will also work.

4 FIX THAT LEAKY ROOF

Never forget to regularly inspect and repair this crucial part of your home. Any leaks when you are surrounded by the dead could quickly become major problems so get them sorted now. More than one zombie siege in history has ended due to supplies being flooded via a leaky roof. Also check your guttering and exterior drains as well as any other flood risks.

5 CREATING A SAFE ROOM

Every zombie survivalist home should have a 'safe room' – a strongly fortified fallback position to which everyone will run if your perimeter is compromised. In most homes, the easiest way to do this is to convert any stairs into a drawbridge style defense which will allow you to seal off the upper floors. If you are in a single-storey dwelling then convert one room into a safe room by reinforcing the interior door and making space for your Bug-Out Bags.

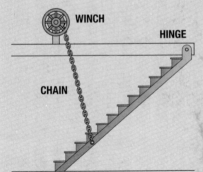

WINCH
HINGE
CHAIN

1 It is a good idea to hire a professional carpenter to create your 'drawbridge stairs' as the workings should be robust and, ideally, the fittings flush.

2 At night or during any breach, once all the survivors have scampered up the stairs, you can raise the drawbridge and effectively seal off the lower floor.

WINCH RAISES THE STAIRS

6 STRENGTHENING AN EXTERIOR FENCE

You must ensure your perimeter is well defended. A horde of zombies can put incredible pressure on your fence – most of it is lateral pressure. If you have the resources then consider fitting a reinforced deep sunk steel fence as outside space will be invaluable during any zombie siege.

1 Surveying your fence, look out for any weak spots including fence posts.

2 Dig in some lateral supports to start with. Focus on fence posts and then other sections.

3 Prepare some pre-mixed concrete, paying careful attention to the water ratios. 2–3 minutes of mixing will be required.

4 Carefully excavate the fence foundations. Distract the zombies when strengthening the foundations with concrete. Do the same for the lateral support.

5 You may want to create a basic 'firestep'. You may now fire at the dead safe in the knowledge that your humble fence has been well and truly constructed!

HOME PREPARATION AND DEFENSE

THE PERFECT ANTI-ZOMBIE HOME

Whether you stayed tucked away in a fortified and isolated log cabin in the woods or stuck in a grimy apartment on the outskirts of a major town, no one location is 100% zombie proof. But in 2009, architects Foster & Webber Associates were commissioned to draw up plans for the world's first affordable anti-zombie family dwelling. A budget of $500,000 was allocated for the new building and although the project did end up costing more, it was never meant to be a fantasy home, with underground bunkers and so on. It was designed as the prototype for mass-produced homes of the future. These are homes which have the added attraction of being zombie resistant, as they are referred to, and this was no flight of fancy; several major house builders who funded the project were responding to data published in the *Property and Real Estate Journal* which indicated that over 63% of home buyers took zombie defense potential into consideration and that for 5% of people, it was the most important consideration in the purchase.

▷ ZOMBIE-RESISTANT HOME

For the ultimate zombie 'prepper', building your home purposely designed to resist the walking dead is the obvious choice, but cost should not be the only consideration. Choosing the right location is also key. Select a building plot too close to, say, a hospital or an army base and you may be overrun despite all of your preparations.

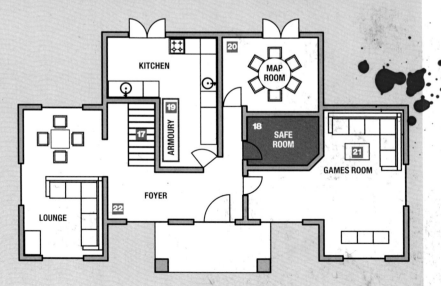

1. Solid external perimeter fence with lateral supports to resist pressure.
2. Razor wire on top of fence.
3. 'Green zone' of safety behind the fence.
4. Vegetable patches.
5. A dug well for extra water.
6. Secure exit and access for vehicles.
7. All windows triple glazing.
8. All lower windows barred.
9. Solid doors to access ground floor.
10. Lookout location from top of house.
11. Heavily insulated roof for cold weather.
12. Chimney and open fires in most rooms.
13. Ample storage space in basement, including sizeable water tank.
14. Rain collection tanks on roof to provide water for washing.
15. Solar panels and wind generators.
16. Emergency diesel generator.

17. Stairs can be lifted to seal off upper floors.
18. Heavily fortified safe room.
19. Secure armory of weapons.

20. Map room – showing foraging locations.
21. Games room for recreation.
22. Bug-Out Bags checked and ready to go at a moment's notice.

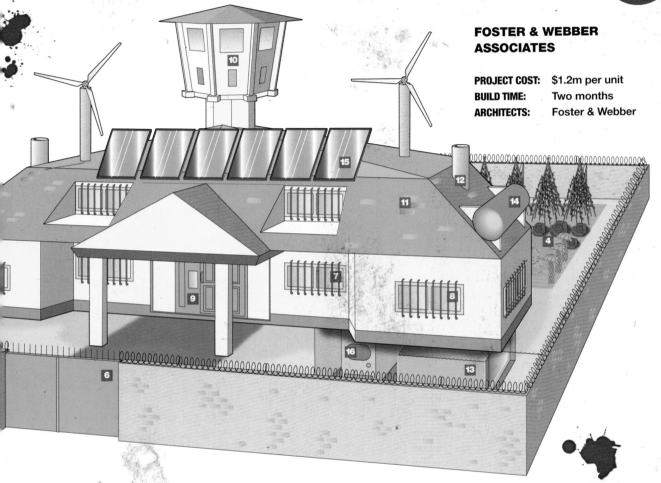

FOSTER & WEBBER ASSOCIATES

PROJECT COST:	$1.2m per unit
BUILD TIME:	Two months
ARCHITECTS:	Foster & Webber

HOME PREPARATION AND DEFENSE
BUYING A NEW HOME

People buying new homes are already beginning to make zombie-defense criteria part of their buying decision. A recent survey revealed that 5% of purchasers see good zombie defense as 'very important', representing a 50% increase on the same survey two years ago.

31% LOCATION
What is the neighborhood like?

15% CONDITION
Is the property well maintained?

14% BEDROOMS
How many bedrooms are there?

2% FAMILY
Is it close to friends and family?

3% TRANSPORT
Where is the nearest bus stop?

5% ZOMBIES
Is this property easily defended against zombies?

8% AMENITIES
How close are the shops, gym?

10% SCHOOLS
How good are the local schools?

12% PARKING
Has it got off-street parking?

SURVEY OF 10,023 PURCHASERS ACROSS THE USA, UK AND GERMANY IN AUGUST 2011

HOME PREPARATION AND DEFENSE

90-DAY RATIONS

A central pillar of the 90-day survival plan is having enough supplies to survive in isolation from the world for the entire period. There is a chance that you could forage an abandoned home after a few weeks, but you should exercise frugality to be self-sufficient in your home fortress in terms of food, water and other supplies.

As a zombie survivalist, you need to start asking some searching questions about your current set-up such as how much food do I currently keep in the house? Do I have a good place to store supplies and, most importantly, do I really think I could last for a few months on one carton of orange juice and a box of cornflakes? More than any part of the 90-day survival plan, laying down stores requires planning and ongoing management. Most items will need to be rotated according to date and you'll need a dry, dark and cool place to store most food items.

Remember to personalize your supplies. If you hate canned peas then there is no reason to ride out the apocalypse almost vomiting every time you force them down. Stock what you enjoy within the main food groups and adjust your stock to take into account any special dietary requirements.

▷ FOOD SUPPLIES

The key in food storage is planning. Firstly, consider the number of survivors you are likely to have, then map out a 3–4 month period of isolation. Secondly, plan the main meal for each day per person. Be conservative with portions and keep a balanced diet for an active person. Don't forget to include treats and to mix things up or there is a risk that after the third straight week of watery gruel, your fellow survivors may be willingly walking into the arms of the hungry dead just to escape your cooking.

EMERGENCY FOOD SUPPLIES

The following items are suggested when selecting emergency food supplies. You may already have many of these to hand.

▶ Ready-to-eat canned meats, fruits, vegetables and a can opener – fresh vegetables will be hard to come by as the distribution network collapses and will be a welcome treat.

▶ Protein or fruit bars will often replace a lunchtime meal. After a busy afternoon bashing zombies, you'll need a snack.

▶ Dried milk powder – the miracle substance and heart of a thousand survival recipes. Ensure you have ample supplies.

▶ Peanut butter packed with the power of this glorious nut, is a great snack on dried biscuits.

▶ Dried fruit – will keep much longer than fresh fruit. Just look at those dried dates you got from an aunt a few years ago – they're still as delicious now as the day you were given them.

▶ Crackers – a great way to boost up any meal and perfect for snacks.

▶ Canned juices – again, you will need these to ensure a balanced diet.

▶ Food for infants – don't forget if your family has little ones or anyone requiring a special diet, you need to plan for this.

Some survival supplies offer a complete 90-day food supply and they range from around $600 per person. You may also opt for dried military rations if you really want to be hardcore.

HOME PREPARATION AND DEFENSE
SELF-SUFFICIENT LIVING

Self-sufficiency living is not just about big-time gardening, it's a whole approach and something you can start implementing immediately. The first step is to identify the key 'inputs' into your home – so we are talking about fruit, vegetables, meat, fish, water, etc. Basically, everything you can currently just go to the supermarket for and top up whenever you please. Self-sufficiency living is about gradually reducing your dependency on these external sources. For example, is there a nearby field with a secure fence which may be suitable for larger scale gardening? Do you have space for a greenhouse which could guarantee you fresh produce all year round and

do you have the necessary skills to catch wild animals such as rabbits to supplement your meat intake? Work to gradually develop your level of self-sufficiency now in preparation for the zombie apocalypse and it won't be such a shock when the dead arrive. Try to build a library of information in areas such as gardening and the smallholder management of livestock. The possibility of catching fish from a nearby river or lake is tempting but depends very much on the number of bodies floating in the water. Most zombie experts expect main waterways to be blocked with the bloated corpses of the dead so you may want to hold the fish for the moment!

FOODS THAT LAST

Here's a handy list of foods that can be stored for over 3 years in the right containers and conditions:

- ▶ Wheat.
- ▶ Vegetable oil.
- ▶ Corn.
- ▶ Baking powder (you can never have enough).
- ▶ Soya beans.
- ▶ Instant coffee, tea.
- ▶ Cocoa (this is a must have).
- ▶ Salt.
- ▶ Non-carbonated soft drinks.
- ▶ White rice.
- ▶ Dry pasta.
- ▶ Powdered milk (in nitrogen-packed cans) – an essential.
- ▶ Apparently, baked beans in a tin can last over 15 years. We're not sure whether this is a comfort or not.
- ▶ Honey and sugar if correctly stored will last for years and liven up many a dull survival meal.
- ▶ Dried apple slices may not sound like much of a treat now but they'll last for years.
- ▶ Dehydrated carrots aren't the tastiest but they do the job.

REMEMBER THE KEY TO KEEPING FOOD IS STORING IT IN THE CORRECT CONDITIONS AND ROTATING YOUR STOCKS!

A FINAL NOTE

Do not be disheartened if you currently have low stocks. Most people today shop on an almost daily basis and are quite used to picking what they want, whenever they want it at the drop of a hat. Start to change your mindset now and build your food stocks up slowly if funds are tight. Create your vegetable patch now and start practicing your survival recipes right away. Any sudden change in diet can be a serious shock to your body – imagine moving your survivor group onto your cabbage-based survival diet only to be driven out of your sealed fortress by the mixture of a non-functioning toilet and the unpleasant vapors from your fellow survivors.

13

▷ WATER

To be on the safe side, you should allocate one gallon (3.8 l) of clean water per adult per day. In purely survival terms, this is generous and other factors such as climate and level of activity will play a part. The 'one gallon a day' calculation includes a small allocation for washing and sanitation. It is important that you should never let your water supply drop below a three-day supply per person in your group.

KEY POINTS ABOUT WATER

1. Commercial firms can provide tanks of over 2000 gallons (7,571 l) if you are serious about securing your supply.
2. Rainwater can be collected for washing or sanitation, but be cautious of water from a stream – always boil it and use a purifier, particularly if it smells a bit 'corpsy'.
3. There is a reservoir of water in the heating system and tanks in most homes – make sure you trap it.
4. When things kick off, run and fill every bath you have in the house – this can provide a useful reserve.
5. Maintain strict water-usage discipline at all times.

5 REASONS WHY SURVIVORS VENTURE INTO ZOMBIETOWN

Any journey into bandit country will be dangerous, but figures collected by the Ministry of Zombies reveal the top five reasons why survivors leave their fortified homes during zombie outbreaks. These findings were based on research into more than 100 documented incidents since 1946.

1. We ran out of water so I went to forage.
2. Food was low and I wanted a bit of variety.
3. I was feeling claustrophobic.
4. I couldn't stand being trapped with those people any longer.
5. I just wanted to get some fresh air.

Apart from the fact that some of these responses are sheer lunacy, running out of water is the number one reason why survivors leave the safety of their shelter and put themselves at risk on the zombie-dominated streets. Clearly, this shows that most survivors seriously underestimated their requirements in terms of water.

OTHER SUPPLIES

Preparing a 90-day survival plan will take time and resources, and when you are on a limited budget it makes sense to concentrate on home fortification, food and water as the priorities. In addition, it's always worth putting a small budget aside for other items – not just the crucial stuff like tools, extra wood, nails and any medicines but also books, games and those little luxuries that make life worth living.

If there are children in the house, consider how you are going to keep them entertained during those long dreary nights – perhaps a collection of classic children's books and toys. Once your e-reader dies out, you'll be back to good old paperbacks so keep a good stock as they can also be useful as kindling for a fire. You can use your powerless e-reader to put plants on, or as a small chopping board.

In addition to these, start building up a library of survival textbooks now – knowledge of first aid, growing your own crops and basic mechanics will become invaluable. It may be an idea to create a 'planning room' in your home where you can store all your books and plans. If you've always wanted one of those rooms you see on TV shows, with photos pinned to the wall and bits of blue string joining things up – this is your chance. Get your survival plans organized and use the planning room for meetings with your survival team. It will help to create the air of seriousness required among the group and make you look like an expert or lunatic depending on the observer.

'DON'T FORGET' ITEMS

Here's a quick 'don't forget' list of essentials put together by a team of survival experts – these are items people typically forget:

▶ **WIND-UP RADIO**

To keep updated with any emergency broadcasts.

▶ **TOILET PAPER**

You'll thank us for this one.

▶ **SHAMPOO**

You can battle the dead and still have coconut fresh hair.

▶ **FIRST AID BOX**

Well-stocked. Check dates on the tablets.

▶ **EXTRA BLANKETS**

For when the heating is out.

▶ **GARBAGE BAGS**

You can never have enough of these.

▶ **MATCHES**

Loads of matches.

▶ **AN ENTERTAINMENT BOX FOR THE KIDS**

Including old board games with pieces missing and old children's books that will put the zombies to sleep.

▶ **ANOTHER BLANKET**

Someone spilt something on the first one.

▶ **WIND-UP TORCH**

These cheap items could be a life saver if you find yourself needing light in an emergency. They aren't very bright but they do the job.

▷ POWER

WHAT HAPPENS WHEN THE LIGHTS GO OUT?

Few people in the developed world live without some form of power in their home and one thing you can be sure of is that once the zombies are in town, it's only a matter of time before the power grid goes down. Survival experts disagree on how long it will last in the aftermath of the apocalypse so it's best to plan for it being out from day one. Invest in a basic portable generator and lay down enough fuel to last you at least a few months. A small generator on average will use about a gallon (3.8 l) a day if used continuously. Below is a list of items you can power with a portable generator (5000 watts per hour)

▶ Central air-conditioning (5000 watts).
▶ X-Box (200 watts).
▶ Standard TV (190 watts).
▶ Computer (120 watts).
▶ Monitor (150 watts).
▶ Laptop (200 watts).
▶ Hot plate (1200 watts).
▶ Oven (3000 watts).
▶ Popcorn popper (1,600 watts).
▶ Average lightbulb (25 watts).
▶ Your illuminated Captain Kirk water feature diorama (7,500 watts of wasted energy).

Obviously, you can't have everything on at once so budget your energy provisions carefully. In addition, a well-lit house amid the darkness will be an open invitation to any bandit out there that you are well supplied and comfortable – expect a visit from your local looters just as your popcorn is popping in the maker. No one knows exactly how long the power will stay on when the dead rise. Research has shown that many of our power stations, including the nuclear ones, can continue for weeks unmanned before auto shutting down. As part of your survival preparations, it is prudent to have several practice weekends without power to really grasp the impact it has on a survival group.

HOME PREPARATION AND DEFENSE

COPING WITH CHILDREN

For families, one of the most challenging tasks will be preparing children for the zombie apocalypse. Depending on their age, they may have some knowledge, but the 'monsters' outside the window will no doubt haunt most for years to come if you don't get that balance right. For example, do you reveal the ugly truth now so that they are pre-warned of the horrors ahead, or sugar-coat it and turn survival training into a fun adventure game? Child psychologists disagree on which approach is best, but simple activities such as keeping children entertained and allocating them small tasks around the home can be a great way to start. Ensure they are involved, keep them updated with developments and, with care, start to train them in the combat skills required to survive.

BUFFO COMIC

In the 1960s, the Ministry of Zombies in London embarked upon an innovative strategy to educate children on the danger of zombies. The comic book *Buffo* – which was published in the USA and the UK between 1963 and 1983, featured a whole series of educational cartoons. They were considered old-fashioned even at the time but were designed to be used by parents to introduce the threat of zombies and ensure that the children understood what to do if they saw one of the walking dead. We have included a favorite classic from 1968 in which an overzealous junior zombie spotter finally manages to stop a major zombie outbreak. You may want to photocopy these – the *Buffo* comics were big sellers in the zombie fighting community right up to when the comic was cancelled in 1983.

Anytown is a quiet suburb but amateur junior detective Annie Riggs is always on the lookout for zombies. This week she can't get out and about on her brand new red bicycle as she's been grounded by Mummy after the

She's looking out of the window

ANNIE: *I can't go out & play today so I'll just sit here zombie spotting. I just know they'll be here today!*

Gosh I'm bored as a bicycle. Hang on, who's that coming up the path?

Annie spots a stranger

ANNIE: *Mother, it's a zombie! He's limping & everything!*

MOTHER: *No dear, that's the postman Frank. He got that limp during the war.*

Soon another visitor approaches

ANNIE: *Mother, it's a zombie. He's staggering all over the place!*

MOTHER: *No dear, that's Albert the gardener. He has sunstroke.*

HOME PREPARATION AND DEFENSE
COPING WITH CHILDREN

CHILDREN AND ZOMBIES DO NOT MIX

The uninformed child can find the lumbering movements and unbalanced gait of zombies humorous and this can lead to serious consequences. Educate your children now. There are many great kids' books out on the market. We have included some classic cartoons from yesteryear.

ARM AS APPROPRIATE

Training is key when any weapons are involved, but your kids must be able to protect themselves. As a rule of thumb, if they are over 10 years old then they should receive a good level of hand weapons training. Younger children may be restricted to the safe areas of your home base. Remember, the world will have changed and your kids need the right skills to survive.

DON'T UNDERESTIMATE LITTLE ONES

Even young children are immensely adaptable and have proved so in countless zombie incidents. Don't overlook them or leave them locked inside if they are keen to contribute. If they are old enough to ask about the zombies then they have the right to know what's going on.

KEEP THINGS FUN

This could apply to everyone. Sure, it's the end of the world as we know it, but keep your child entertained with games, books and things to do. A humorous game of 'who can spot the funniest zombie' can help kill the hours during a zombie siege. Ensure that your supplies include plenty of creative things to do. It's boredom that will cause most problems so prepare now.

trouble she caused by reporting her elderly neighbors, Mr & Mrs Arkwright, for being Russian spies – turns out they were just going on vacation! The long school holidays are really beginning to drag for Annie and she can't wait to go out exploring again but soon her day is going to be interrupted by some rather odd strangers!

Annie is most unhappy

ANNIE: I just know the zombies are out there and I need to keep Anytown safe. I know – I'll get my Bumper Book of the Dead I got for Christmas!

Now in place with her book, she sees another figure staggering up the path.

Annie checks her book

ANNIE: Righto, staggering, yes, limping yes, blood thirsty look, yes. This has just got to be one, it just has to be! Mum! There's a zombie in the garden!

Mother is busy in the kitchen and does not believe her. Annie runs to the hallway and dials the Police.

Officer Bumble congratulates Annie

OFFICER BUMBLE: Well done young lady. We always keep an eye out for 'odd sorts' & catching this zombie before it could do any more damage was just fantastic!

ANNIE: It's all thanks to my Bumper Book of the Dead!

17

HOME PREPARATION AND DEFENSE

HOW TO SURVIVE A ZOMBIE SIEGE

The few first weeks of the zombie apocalypse will be open season for the walking dead. The unprepared will be stuck in their cars on blocked highways. Looters will be breaking into shops, oblivious to the risks around them. Hungry survivors with inadequate food supplies will soon be driven on to the streets foraging.

However, this 'time of plenty' will not last for the zombies and they will eventually turn their attention to the remaining survivors as they cower, fortified within their homes. Picture it: you wake up one day, look outside only to find a sea of dead eyes looking hungrily back at you. It could be hundreds. It could even be thousands. You are under zombie siege and you need to be prepared for the challenge.

There are four key interlinking strategies to surviving a zombie siege:

1 KEEPING DISCIPLINE
You must maintain order and control within the group to survive

2 STAYING STRONG
Personal fitness is important. Regularly check your defenses

3 RESOURCE MANAGEMENT
Start tracking your supplies from day one of the siege

4 HAVE A PLAN B
Always prepare an escape plan or plans from any situation

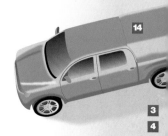

SIEGE STRATEGIES

Providing you have the supplies, or can at least sneak out to top up essential items, most well-fortified sites will be able to last indefinitely against the dead. There is always a chance that the zombies will become distracted by easier meals elsewhere.

However, if the dead maintain their vigil and your supplies are down to a week or less then you should consider a breakout. This complex maneuver will involve some careful planning.

1 You should use any distraction techniques you can to divert the dead from your intended exit.

2 The whole group should be ready with their Bug-Out Bags and weapons.

3 Everyone should know the agreed Bug-Out location. You may choose to scatter in different directions, but be precise on where to meet up.

SURVIVING A ZOMBIE SIEGE

▶ Monitoring and reinforcing your fortifications must be your first priority. Remember to fortify in a systematic fashion so that if one layer is overrun, you simply fall back.

▶ Manage your resources from day one. Ration food and water. Maintain strict discipline on supplies and supplement with rainwater and food you've grown.

▶ Start planning an escape route. Useful options can be across roofs or through lofts into neighboring houses.

▶ Enforce a Daily Work Schedule – you must keep the besieged busy for at least 4–5 hours per day. Activities can include strengthening defenses or perimeter patrol.

▶ Keep young survivors occupied with a range of games and activities.

▶ Invest in some ear plugs – the relentless drone of the dead can have a detrimental effect on the besieged, particularly at night.

▶ Lessons from Churchill – you must maintain a 100% belief that you will all make it through. Never let your fellow survivors see you questioning this assumption.

UNDER SIEGE

1. Reinforced fencing checked regularly with increasing pressure.
2. Fellow survivor working on an escape route just in case.
3. Distracting techniques being used.
4. A skilled slinger taking pot shots to help manage boredom.
5. Off-duty survivors playing a board game and relaxing.
6. Earplugs – survivors sleeping soundly
7. Guard duty – a clear rota system.
8. Schedule on the wall – tasks for at least 4–5 hours a day.
9. Food and supplies checked and regularly audited. Rations managed.
10. Bug-Out Bags ready to go.
11. Doors reinforced.
12. A survivor gardening to keep up morale and food stocks. Also catching pigeons.
13. A survivor on a radio listening in case help is within reach.
14. Possible break-out vehicle on standby.
15. All windows have been barred and have steel shutters to create an additional perimeter.

HOME PREPARATION AND DEFENSE

SURVIVAL LOCATIONS

Whether you are a well-prepared zombie survivalist, with a robust 90-day plan to get you through the zombie apocalypse or someone who plans to 'take it as it comes' when the dead arrive, you will need to consider the best locations to hold out in. For many, their own home or apartment will be the logical choice whereas the unprepared may find themselves caught at school or in the office as the dead come a munching. Working with a group of seasoned zombie survival experts, the Ministry of Zombies has produced the following analysis of typical survivor locations. Each profile includes a brief overview, followed by a breakdown of the advantages and disadvantages in terms of zombie defense. Remember, this is general advice. The sites will vary greatly according to factors ranging from proximity to the epicentre of the zombie outbreak and population density to country and climate. Many of the home fortification guidelines outlined above will serve the survivor equally well for these sites.

OTHER KEY FACTORS

Another key factor to consider is access to your chosen survival location. If you live close to the wilderness or a National Park then an isolated survival location might be within scope for you and your family. After all, with the warnings from your monitoring system, you'll be able to pack up and leave before the stories of people being eaten even hit our television screens. However, if you are in a city center then the chaos will spread quicker once the word gets out and you don't want to be caught in miles of jammed traffic, in a car packed with supplies. You may as well put a neon sign on the car saying 'Please come and loot my supplies'.

Think carefully about access to any long-term survival locations. Many zombie survivalists plan to spend the first few months of the crisis in their own fortified homes before moving out to their longer term site once the initial chaos has died down. Remember, for this to work you'll need multiple routes and a well-researched travel plan as you and your group of survivors will be moving through the zombie-infested territory. Review the options on the next few pages and make your own notes. Decide whether you need a long-term location – consider factors such as water supply, food sources and the overall sustainability of your primary location. Any travel will be dangerous, particularly if you have family or survivors with limited mobility.

▶ RESIDENTIAL SITE

POKING AROUND OTHER PEOPLE'S HOMES

The easiest option when looking for a site to escape the zombies, particularly if you are caught out in the open, will be residential sites, but will the residents still be there? And, will they be human? An apartment block could be a perfect survival location with multiple flats to loot for supplies.

ADVANTAGES

▶ These sites are most common and with thousands fleeing the chaos, there will be no shortage of empty homes for you to explore.

▶ You can select a good defensive location, with a decent perimeter wall and other key zombie defense features such as double-glazing and a strong front door.

▶ It's a chance to live in the neighborhood you've always wanted to.

▶ If you seal the ground floor and entrance of an apartment block, you can work your way methodically through the apartments, securing supplies as you go. You may also be able to link up with other survivors and work on a plan to defend the block as a community.

DISADVANTAGES

▶ The original occupants may not be thrilled to see you busting through their window and threatening to take their supplies.

▶ The original occupants may be more interested in feasting on your flesh. Be prepared for terrible odors if you break into a 'dead house'.

▶ Many homes will be poorly set up in terms of zombie defense – if it had been on the owner's list of priorities then they probably wouldn't have fled.

SUITABILITY 👍👍👍👍👍

▶ POLICE STATION

DIAL 911 TO SURVIVE THE ZOMBIES?

With dozens of officers, many of them armed, a fortified location at the center of any anti-zombie actions and a dedicated force of men and women ready to serve and protect – the humble city police station sounds like the ideal location to hold out against the dead.

ADVANTAGES

▶ Likely to be the focus on any fight back against the dead in the first days of a zombie crisis.

▶ A good stock of firearms, ammunition and riot gear.

▶ Typically these sites are well-fortified, with barred lower windows and secure cells.

▶ A disciplined group of trained officers will make up an ideal early survivor group.

▶ A police station is the ideal place to start fighting the dead. It is likely that a cadre of officers will already be planning to start.

DISADVANTAGES

▶ Most stations will be on the frontline of the fight so expect infected individuals to be 'brought in for questioning' in the confusion before the word 'zombie' is used.

▶ Stations may be abandoned as officers flee to protect their own families and will become key sites for gangs and other aggressive looters looking for guns and other booty.

▶ These sites don't stock much in the way of food. Survivors cannot live on doughnuts alone.

SUITABILITY 👍👍👍👍👍

▶ THE OFFICE

END OF THE WORLD AND YOU'RE AT WORK

Picture it. It's a typical day at work. You are battling through a mountain of emails, only to be told that the dead are now feasting on the living outside. There is too much chaos to attempt the commute home and you are only armed with a half-full stapler and a degree in Business Studies.

ADVANTAGES

▶ Strong main doors should be easy enough to fortify. Don't forget to blockade the fire exits.

▶ Some buildings have their own emergency generators.

▶ Most office buildings now have a plethora of security features including shatter proof glass and CCTV.

▶ An open office layout may encourage creative solutions to battling the dead. You will also have a good supply of flipcharts and stationary so you can 'brainstorm' your way out of trouble.

DISADVANTAGES

▶ Most offices are built as shells and use weak plasterboard partitions to create internal rooms. These walls will not hold back the hungry hordes.

▶ Panicking work colleagues may not be the ideal material for your survivor group.

▶ Food will be limited to the moldy remnants in the office fridge. Where there is a cafeteria, there may be more supplies.

▶ Do you really want to be trapped at work when the end of the world finally comes?

SUITABILITY 👍👍👍👍👍

HOME PREPARATION AND DEFENSE

▶ SHOPPING MALL

THE CLASSIC ZOMBIE SURVIVAL LOCATION

The latest fashions, acres of shop space and more coffee shops than a small city, a modern shopping mall offers some enticing options to a zombie survivalist. It's a legendary location to defend, made famous in movies/training films such as *Dawn of the Dead*.

ADVANTAGES

- ▶ Clothing, supplies and even firearms will be plentiful with multiple food outlets providing useful sources of food.
- ▶ Most modern shopping centers are flooded with natural light which will be useful if the electricity shuts down. Many also have their own electricity-generating capacity.
- ▶ There may be green space for you to start growing your own food.
- ▶ There is always plenty of parking and this will only get better during a zombie apocalypse.

DISADVANTAGES

- ▶ It would take a small army to secure the literally hundreds of doors and fire escapes. Maybe they were all locked when you arrived but you can't take that chance.
- ▶ These locations typically attract thousands of visitors and employ hundreds of people on site. If they're still there as zombies, a shopping mall will be a dangerous place to clear.
- ▶ A shopping mall is the number one location on every looter and bandit's list. It is not a question of if you have to defend the site against human raiders, it's a question of when.

▶ INDUSTRIAL SITE

A LONG SHIFT WILL MAKE THESE SITES SAFE

It's 8:10 AM and you have just punched in 10 minutes late for your shift. But, good news. Your supervisor has been savaged by the dead on her way to work and half the staff are currently being mauled in the car park. Surviving the zombies in a factory or warehouse will present both challenges and opportunities.

ADVANTAGES

- ▶ Most sites will have a robust external security fence which can be sealed to create a secure perimeter.
- ▶ Any office areas are great locations to set up your 'home base' and cafeteria areas will provide good sources of supplies.
- ▶ Any roof tanks could provide a useful supply of water but always boil it before drinking.
- ▶ Many factories are well stocked with tools and other raw materials so there'll be no shortage of hand weapons such as hammers.

DISADVANTAGES

- ▶ A complex and confusing layout with multiple exits is not the easiest location to defend.
- ▶ The sheer size of these sites can make securing them a challenge.
- ▶ If horror movies have taught us anything, it is that most factories abound with hanging chains with a tendency to rust easily and move around in a spooky way, clinking as if something has just passed. No one wants that.
- ▶ These sites typically have large delivery doors which, if breached, could allow the dead to flood in.

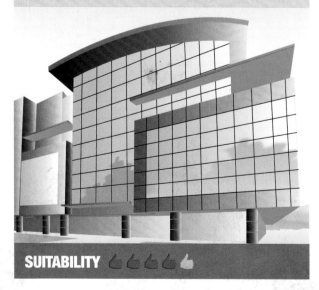

SUITABILITY 👍👍👍👍👍

SUITABILITY 👍👍👍👍👍

▶ PRISON

LOCKED UP MAY BE THE BEST PLACE TO BE

Well-fortified and secure, purpose-built modern prisons present some interesting opportunities and challenges to zombie survivalists. Ensure that you have scouted a prison before the zombies arrive if you intend to use it as a settlement location, preferably as a visitor rather than a permanent resident!

ADVANTAGES

▶ A robust external perimeter fence designed to keep people out as well as in. Add in guard towers and the ability to seal off areas and the modern prison complex is an easily defensible site.

▶ The location will include an armory of weapons used by guards such as riot gear and firearms.

▶ Prisons have extensive catering, food and other facilities such as laundry etc. You will not be short of supplies in one of these locations.

DISADVANTAGES

▶ An interesting choice of either hundreds of dangerous criminals still locked in their cells after the guards have fled or legions of the infected hidden in endless corridors and dead ends.

▶ These sites will be first choice locations for any 'ex-cons' looking to start as a Robber Baron in the new world. Expect hordes of villains as well as the dead.

▶ Sprawling sites with hundreds of doors and locks may prove too much for smaller survivor groups.

SUITABILITY 👍👍👍👍👍

▶ BUNKER

SECRET BUNKER – WHAT COULD BE BETTER?

Whether you are buried deep in an underground shelter or defended by 6-foot (1.8- m) thick reinforced concrete, one thing is sure: neither zombies nor looters will be able to break into a sealed bunker easily. Once inside, you'll be safe and trapped in with the other survivors, or even alone. Remember to take a book.

ADVANTAGES

▶ They don't come much more secure than this. Once you seal that steel blast door, you are safe from virtually all attackers. Safe and sound, trapped in your bunker. That's good isn't it?

▶ A well-stocked bunker will be capable of supplying you with food, water and energy for years to come. You could hide there and wait for the whole thing to blow over.

▶ With a hidden entrance, no one is going to find you.

DISADVANTAGES

▶ Studies have shown that humans struggle with being 'trapped' underground for long periods of time. The lack of natural sunlight, fresh air and the development of 'cabin fever' are all potential risks.

▶ If you are sealed in a bunker or any location with the wrong people, it could be like being stuck in a never-ending episode of the *Kardashians* – with insanity and madness slowly developing.

▶ Simply hiding from the zombies won't make them go away. You could emerge after a year only to find millions of zombies in a land of the dead waiting to feast on you.

SUITABILITY 👍👍👍👍👍

HOME PREPARATION AND DEFENSE

▷ BOAT

A LIFE ON THE WAVES AWAY FROM DANGER

The option of living aboard a boat during a zombie outbreak has its attractions as you'd be away from the clawing hands of the dead and the violence and chaos as society crumbles. Zombies cannot swim but they do drift and bodies can float so you'll be safer apart from the risk of a ghoul clambering aboard.

ADVANTAGES

▶ Zombies have trouble with water. Apart from the danger of the odd floating dead, you'll be safe from the hordes off shore.
▶ Using a dinghy, you can make foraging trips ashore for supplies.
▶ Choose the right vessel and you could be set up for months. For example, a commercial whaler will cost around $300,000, has room for 15–20 survivors and can cover over 20,000 nautical miles (23,016 miles/37,040 km) on a single tank of fuel.

DISADVANTAGES

▶ At some point, you will need a land base for repairs, refuelling and supplies. Any serious damage to the boat could leave you and your survivor group in serious trouble.
▶ Many zombie survivalists favoring an escape by boat carefully make their plans and stock their craft only to ignore the fact that they will need to reach the vessels when the dead rise. Moreover, the chances are that the first panicky survivor who spots it in the marina will try to make off with it.
▶ It is estimated that piracy will increase exponentially during any zombie crisis.

▷ MILITARY BASE

FIREPOWER TO DEFEAT THE WALKING DEAD?

Under the right leadership, military bases will become powerful bastions of humanity as the living battle the hordes of the dead. Could joining the army as they fight to survive be the best move, particularly if you live close to one of their bases? Bases could also become the focus of any human resistance against the zombies.

ADVANTAGES

▶ Well-armed and trained soldiers. Stockpiles of weapons and ammunition. The mouth-watering prospect of tanks and other armored vehicles – with this kind of power, you can really take the war to the zombies.
▶ Most military sites have substantial stocks of tasteless c-rations or tinned 'combat meals'.
▶ These locations tend to be fortified with steel fences as an exterior barrier together with watch towers and controlled access points.

DISADVANTAGES

▶ Thousands of desperate civilians will make for these sites. Expect long lines as people are checked and massive traffic jams as the unprepared flock for the protection of the military.
▶ Some zombie survival experts predict that the military will disintegrate as the dead overrun the country, leaving only dangerous armed groups guarding these locations.
▶ There is a high likelihood that some rogue General will declare 'martial law' as the crisis develops and the discipline may become worse than a North Korean Summer Camp.

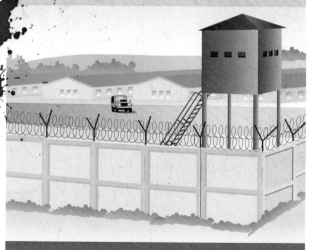

SUITABILITY 👍👍👍👍👍

SUITABILITY 👍👍👍👍

► THE WILDERNESS

AWAY FROM THE HUSTLE AND BUSTLE

If you have access to a wilderness location, then getting away from urban concentrations will certainly help you dodge the hordes of dead that will be ravaging the streets. Key to this location will be access – have a good plan so that you get away before the rush to avoid that whole 'traffic jam bloodbath' scene.

ADVANTAGES

► Once well away from any main towns, cities or roads – you will be relatively safe from both zombies and any human attackers.
► Plenty of 'alone time' and the benefits of plenty of fresh air.
► You will have a chance to use all of that expensive camping and hiking gear you bought a few years ago.
► Growing a long beard can help you create a cool 'mountain man' look – providing you are male and have a chequered shirt.

DISADVANTAGES

► Surviving without hot showers may start to wear thin as winter sets in.
► Food can be scarce unless you have the hunting, fishing or foraging skills to provide for yourself and your group.
► You will need an excellent level of fitness and survival training to stay alive in winter or in hostile climates such as the jungle or desert.
► You will need to be able to cope with any medical emergency yourself or within the group. Fancy having a tooth out with only a handful of lingenberries as an anaesthetic?

SUITABILITY 👍👍👍👍👍

► DESERT ISLAND

A TROPICAL PARADISE FREE OF ZOMBIES

Cutting yourself off from the world can be appealing at the best of times. Add to that several million flesh-eating corpses and a tropical island starts to look like a very attractive proposition. You'll be away from those cold winters and you may even decide to build a house on the beach, complete with monkey waiters.

ADVANTAGES

► Complete zombie-free living in a tropical paradise location.
► Miles of golden sand and warm weather all year round, creating a holiday-like atmosphere for you and your survivor group.
► If you have a small boat, you can raid the mainland or nearby islands for those extra essentials.
► An endless supply of coconuts if it's a tropical island.

DISADVANTAGES

► An endless supply of coconuts and seafood. This is bad news if you don't like coconuts or seafood.
► There is a small risk that a stray corpse will wash up on your golden sands as you lay sunbathing.
► How in the world are you going to get there? Direct flights will be hard to come by after the zombie apocalypse.
► If you make it, being cut off from the world has its downsides. Your social life will certainly tail off.
► If you think your island is a paradise, so will others. Soon, your monkey waiters could be serving drinks to some cruel pirate as you are working in the fields to grow your new masters more food.

SUITABILITY 👍👍👍👍👍

THE PERFECT ZOMBIE-PROOF LOCATION

No Man's Land Fort was built in the 1860's off the coast of Portsmouth, England. Originally constructed to defend against French invaders, it has now been converted into a luxury hotel with more than 20 rooms, two helipads and a heated indoor swimming pool. The fort is about a mile (1.6 km) from the mainland and rises over 60 feet (18 m) above the sea. At today's prices, it would cost around $150 million to build.

Whilst no one site could ever be said to be the perfect zombie-proof location, this fort comes close and with an additional expenditure of around $25 million, it could be transformed into the zombie-proof fortress below. Remember, you may be able to source a similar primary site wherever you are in the world and several zombie-fighting groups are looking at 'crowd funding' their own perfect zombie hideouts. You will need a good sized site with obvious zombie-proofing potential, but it need not be a purpose-designed fortification. It could be an old factory with a particularly strong exterior fence, or an isolated hotel with plenty of space for growing your own crops. What is shown here is simply an example of what can be achieved.

CROWD FUNDING A ZOMBIE FORTRESS

Investing in the creation of an ideal anti-zombie fortress will doubtless cost millions. It doesn't matter if you buy some isolated plot of land in the Australian outback or convert a historic sea fort – you will require substantial financial resources to complete a grand plan like this. Many sites will come as a shell in terms of zombie defense, meaning that you will need to add on the costs of improving the site as well as the initial purchase.

However, it is possible to join forces with other zombie survivalists and 'crowd fund' a defensive site. This means developing a group of friends or family who commit resources to a central fund and this is then used to create your zombie outbreak hideaway. You can find out more about these funds on many of the zombie survival forums on the internet. One group of survivalists in Glasgow has already purchased an island off the West Coast of Scotland and is currently constructing a village of ten homes with a surrounding steel fence. The group also has a boat in Glasgow which they plan to use as part of their Bug-Out plan. It will shuttle to and from the port taking survivors to their long-term settlement location. At least that's the theory!

DEVELOPING A 'SURVIVAL NARRATIVE'

A survey by *Survivor Magazine* revealed that whilst 78% of respondents who had a prepared long-term location felt they have detailed plans on how to reach their secure basis in crisis, less than 23% had any real plan on what they were going to do as the weeks of isolation dragged on. Few were able to answer the underlying question – 'what's the long-term plan once you reach your fortress?' Family members and fellow survivors will start to ask what the plan is and how long you can last. You may not have all the answers but you need to have a 'survival narrative' which provides them with some level of response and you need to be consistent in this area.

▶ 'ONCE WE ARE IN OUR SECURE FORTRESS, WE WILL RUN SILENT FOR THE FIRST MONTH OF THE CRISIS. THIS TIME WILL BE ABOUT STOCK TAKING, SECURING OUR POSITION AND SEEING OUT THE INITIAL CHAOS OF THE OUTBREAK.'
Be firm here, don't be pressured into moving too fast – there will be countless rumors of safe zones and many of these will be just rumors. Ensure that the group understands the danger of being 'out on the road'.

▶ 'AFTER THIS PERIOD, WE WILL REVIEW THE SITUATION AND CONSIDER SENDING OUT FACT-FINDING PATROLS OR SCOUTS IF IT'S SAFE TO DO SO. YOU MAY BE ABLE TO MONITOR EMERGENCY BROADCASTS AND GET THIS INFORMATION.'
Be sure that you do not alert other desperate survivors to your safe location unless you have the resources to take more people in.

▶ 'OUR LONG-TERM PLAN IS TO STAY SECURE IN THE BUNKER FOR AT LEAST 90 DAYS AND TO REVIEW LONGER TERM OPTIONS DURING THIS PERIOD. IF WE CAN EXPAND OUR CURRENT LOCATION THEN WE MAY USE IT AS A LONG-TERM SETTLEMENT LOCATION. IF NOT, WE WILL CONSIDER ONE OF THE ALPHA SITES ALREADY IDENTIFIED.'
Again, be clear and decisive on this. Fellow survivors will raise all sorts of crazy ideas which will almost certainly involve your group heading off in bandit country on a fool's errand.

Build your survival narrative around these kinds of statements. Survivors will be scared enough as it is so any degree of security you can provide will be welcome. Remember, you may not have all the answers, you may not even believe 100% in what you're saying but as a leader you will need to stay strong and adapt as required.

NO MAN'S LAND FORT

1. Mounted M60s placed strategically around the fort to defend against pirates.
2. Over sixty feet (18 m) above sea level so no zombie can clamber up and so protect the fort from rough seas.
3. A secured launch for raiding the mainland for supplies and searching for survivors.
4. A helicopter and helipad, perfect for longer range air patrols. Kit also includes several heli-drones which can be flown over the mainland.
5. Extensive roof gardens and greenhouses for fresh fruit and vegetables, protected from sea-spray by toughened glass
6. 10 foot (3 m) thick concrete walls, able to resist all small arms fire and many other guns and missiles.

7. A fully-equipped hydroelectric generator deep within the fort.
8. Aviation fuel for the helicopter and a full stock of spare parts.
9. Command tower which can also be sealed if the fort is over-run, allowing secure access to the helipad.
10. A fully equipped armory and workshop.
11. Living quarters for up to 100 within the fort, including a cafeteria and medical bay.
12. A radar guided anti-missile gun – controlled from the command post.
13. A defensive array of surface to surface missiles to target hostile vessels or locations on the mainland.

14. A secure walkway for armed foot patrols and lookouts.
15. An expansive reinforced glass dome to maximize natural light within the fort interior.
16. Fort is built using a rocky outcrop as a foundation, over two miles (3.2 km) from the coast.
17. A fresh water bore hole has been sunk into the rock below the fort and now provides the sea-fort with drinking water.
18. A satellite and listening dish monitors world events as well as getting updates from any satellites still operational.
19. A glass conservatory with a library and comfortable chairs for relaxing.
20. A fully equipped communications center which also doubles as a cinema complex for survivors.

SURVIVING THE APOCALYPSE

The 90-Day Survival Plan is just that – it's designed to get you through the first months of the crisis. However, once you reach Day 50 of the zombie apocalypse, you will need to turn your attention to linking up with other survivors.

It's not just about surviving; you need to take charge and build a survivor community capable of defending itself against any bandit groups as well as the walking dead.

Your first steps may be to send a lone scout to the immediate surrounding areas. Who has survived? Can you work together? Maybe you have friends in the local area? To survive in the long term, your group must expand, but it will always be a judgment call on who you can trust.

As a general rule, by Day 50 you should consider linking up with other survivors. The initial chaos will have died down, with maybe just hardcore looters and a few surviving human groups out there. Expect to see zombies on every street, wandering aimlessly as their primary food source becomes more scarce. You can start small in the beginning but you should be planning for a few months down the line and establishing a major survivor colony.

The ideal set-up is to link with families and other survivors in your street or local area. You should establish yourself as leader. The expert knowledge you have picked up from this manual will help reinforce you as the obvious choice. You know what's happened, how it happened and what's going to happen next!

▷ A SURVIVOR CAMP – DAY 100

If your community has just settled in a suburban location then linking up a street or cul-de-sac may be the easiest way to provide a secure location. Other examples could include a large high-rise building or city block. There may be occasions when your current set-up is just not suitable for longer-term settlement. It will be dangerous transiting through zombie-infested areas, but some options and guidelines will be reviewed later.

1 Armed guards patrol keep points and the perimeter at all times. They work in 4-hour shifts and are looking out for both zombie and human threats.

2 The main entrance is blocked with two large buses, each with extra metal mesh welded onto the sides. They are simply reversed to open the route in for vehicles.

3 Regular patrols are out checking on the local area, looking for survivors and foraging for supplies. It's a dangerous job and these teams will soon become battle hardened.

4 A main residential block has been cleared and made secure for survivors. For the moment, everyone sleeps in the same block for security reasons.

5 An area for official notices and a notice board in which survivors can look out for anyone they know. Jobs and missions are also advertised here.

6 This secure area is known as the green zone and includes a small yard for survivors to enjoy. People need some escape from the constant tension and threats.

7 The whole perimeter of this small area has been checked and sealed. The survivors have used several buildings and a central courtyard to create a much bigger survivor settlement.

8 New survivors are still being found and go through a structured induction into camp life. Everyone has a role and everyone is expected to contribute.

9 A field canteen provides hot and cold food 24 hours a day as fighters and camp workers often work shifts. This is where they can relax and catch up on camp gossip.

10 A fortified command bunker from where the camp leader can supervise a growing community.

11 Foraged supplies are documented and stored in these containers. For example, the survivors are already stockpiling sweaters and coats for the winter months.

DEFENSE AND PERIMETER

Establish a defensive perimeter around your community. Clear the interior and then fortify. Use any existing barriers you can, for example, you can block the back of homes and use them as a wall.

FOOD AND WATER

You should gather all supplies together as soon as possible. Prevent individuals from hoarding food. You need to ascertain your current level of provision and create a communal food kitchen.

ALLOCATE ROLES

This can be ad-hoc at first but you will need a rota system for guard duty, kitchen duty, etc. Audit the skills of your community and have crucial areas such as medical training covered.

POOL YOUR WEAPONS

You need to establish that you can defend your new community. Distribute weapons to your guards and create hand weapons for all survivors. Everyone should carry a weapon.

SCOUTS AND FORAGERS

Scouts should be sent out to map the local area and source for any urgent supplies. Your foraging teams should stay close and concentrate only on what your community needs.

ALWAYS LOOK TO EXPAND YOUR SETTLEMENT FURTHER BY SEARCHING FOR NEW SURVIVORS – HUMANITY WILL BE RELYING ON YOU – NO PRESSURE!

SURVIVING THE APOCALYPSE

SURVIVOR INTEGRATION

Many of the survivors your scouts pick up will be shell-shocked, frightened and desperate. However, you should not simply introduce new members into your group without due process.

At the start, your integration process may be ad-hoc and consist of a brief medical check and a chat over a coffee. However, as soon as you have the resources, you should structure the process to cope with increasing numbers of refugees in an organized way.

The Survivor Integration Model was designed by the

Ministry of Zombies for just this purpose. It is a three-stage plan to incorporate people safely into your team. It is based on the core principle that these groups of individuals must be virus-free, safe to join your group and willing to sign up to your rules.

As leader, there will be some tough decisions ahead, one of which will be turning people away. What if they don't want to be part of your group? What if they look like 'trouble'? You will need to be a firm-but-fair leader. Making the hard choices comes with the territory.

SURVIVOR INTEGRATION MODEL	STAGE 1 CLEARING	STAGE 2 INDUCTION	STAGE 3 INTEGRATION
	Check that the new incumbents are virus free, and can safely be released into the community	Make clear the rules of the settlement and how to access essential services. Also, audit their skills	New survivors are allocated roles within the community according to their abilities and offered a mentor

STAGE 1
CLEARING

This first stage of the Survivor Integration Model is the important one – it includes your initial contact with the newcomers and will set the tone for the whole process through to their becoming a fully fledged member of your community. Ideally, your initial contact point should be away or at least outside of your main site. In most cases, your teams will be bringing in survivors they have found while out on patrols. The people they find will be frightened and suspicious, so ensure that they know exactly what is going to happen. It may be useful to have some refreshments ready as they come in to the waiting area. The main objective of the Clearing stage is to process the newcomers through until they are ready to start their formal induction process. So this includes initial contact, first interview and then a period of 24–48 hours in isolation.

NEVER RUSH TO PROCESS NEW SURVIVORS – IT ONLY TAKES ONE INFECTED INDIVIDUAL TO DESTROY YOUR SURVIVOR SETTLEMENT!

CLEARING 1
ESCORT TO CLEARING

A group of new survivors is discovered and escorted into a clearing station. They are welcomed but kept under guard for the moment. Your teams should provide food, water and shelter if required. If some survivors are clearly ill-suited to your settlement then you should escort them away from the clearing station.

STAGE 2
INDUCTION

This stage is about ensuring they understand the rules of the settlement and are thoroughly briefed on any intelligence of the zombies, other survivor communities and foraging sites.

- ☑ We, the survivors, do pledge ourselves to building a safe and fair community.

- ☑ We will welcome others where it is safe to do so and work together, sharing the load and duties.

- ☑ We are dedicated to defeating the zombie menace in all its forms.

- ☑ We will battle bandits and those opposed to the above with everything we have.

- ☑ We pledge to obey our community commander until the end of the zombie war. At this time, we will facilitate and support a return to democracy.

By joining this community, you agree to abide by the charter of this settlement.

STAGE 3
INTEGRATION

Once survivors have signed up they can be integrated fully into the community. This will mean having work and tasks allocated to them according to their skills and abilities. The process needs to include showing new arrivals the essentials around the base. They should have quarters allocated, know what time they are due at the canteen and have any defensive duties assigned.

TYPICAL INTEGRATION DAY
1. Tour of the base perimeter.
2. Talk through the rules and regulations.
3. Allocation of quarters.
4. In-depth intelligence debrief.
5. In-depth skills audit.
6. Commander meeting.
7. Final ceremony.

SURVIVORS MUST SIGN UP OR MOVE ON!

CLEARING 2
INTERVIEW

They enter a sealed area of your settlement. They are checked over by a medic and interviewed. Importantly, survivors must never feel like they've been arrested. At any time, they must be free to walk out of the process. However, they should not be allowed within your bases without going through clearing.

CLEARING 3
ISOLATION

The zombie virus is hard to isolate in the blood so as a precaution survivors are put in isolation pens for 48 hours. It is vital that new survivors keep to the rules and regulations of the settlement. You should have an internal militia force to manage law and order as your base of operations grows.

SURVIVING THE APOCALYPSE

THE USEFUL ZOMBIE

It will come as no surprise to many that government and international organizations around the world have already spent millions on studies to find a use for the walking dead. The United Nations feasibility report 455/AA is one such document and has been widely leaked across the internet. One of its declared objectives was:

> **TO PROVIDE INSIGHT INTO THE POSSIBLE UTILITY WHICH CAN BE MADE OF THOSE SUFFERING FROM THE ZOMBIC CONDITION, TAKING INTO FULL ACCOUNT THEIR EXEMPTION FROM THE UNITED NATIONS DECLARATION OF HUMAN RIGHTS BY AMENDMENT 40122A TO THE AFOREMENTIONED DOCUMENT**

UNITED NATIONS DOCUMENT ON ZOMBIC USAGE 455/AA OCTOBER 2007

Riveting stuff eh? But in a nation dominated by the walking dead, are there ways in which we can harness the power of the zombie for the benefit of all survivors?

ZOMBIES AS FOOD – A WARNING FROM HISTORY

In the small village of Del Peiro in Southern Italy in 1864, one very troubled priest sought to fight off the famine blighting his congregation by 'harvesting' zombies.

Father Claudio Baldini went on to produce a twisted document known as the *Zombie Cookbook*. It detailed how the living could take choice cuts from the dead and, with the right preparation and seasoning, prepare a palatable food source. Fragments of the book are said to remain in the Vatican Library and several pages are available online. The official Ministry of Zombies line states that in no way are zombies safe to eat. No cuts from a ghoul may be prepared in any way that would make them safe.

There are plenty of animals and possibly even people who would be classed as carrion-eaters – that is, they feed on the corpses of the dead as their main source of energy. Vultures are some of the most famous examples in the bird kingdom, but many insects and animals rely on things such as 'road kill' to survive. Now, in a world dominated by zombies, food will become increasingly scarce. It is estimated that survivors will have enough canned and dried food for a few years, but after this and unless we start to grow and harvest crops again, food will become increasingly scarce. There have been episodes of using the walking dead as a potential source of food throughout history.

WARNING – DO NOT EAT ZOMBIES!

1 POWER GENERATION

Any zombie power-generation machine must take into account the fact that zombies generally require 'motivation' for them to move. This is most often the scent of human flesh or blood. This principle is employed in the simple zombie power-generation design shown here, which illustrates how, with even a limited set-up, you can generate electricity to support your community. You won't have enough power to turn the air-conditioning back on, but working with 16 zombies on 12-hour shifts you should be able to generate enough power for lighting and basic cooking.

2 ZOMBIES AS FUEL

Nothing burns as well as dried zombies so, providing there has been no heavy rain and you are in an area of low humidity, the option of burning zombies for either power generation, warmth or just for the fun of it is worth considering. In terms of power generation, you are looking mainly at fuelling steam-power generators – imagine where coal was once used, you now just chuck on another corpse. Burning corpses is of course good practice anyway to restrict the spread of pests and the virus itself.

3 ZOMBIES FOR TRANSPORT

Again using the principle of 'motivation', it is possible to utilize a team of zombies to pull a simple cart or wagon. However, before getting carried away, be mindful that this idea relies on a regular supply of fresh human flesh.

⚠ **NEVER RIDE A ZOMBIE**

YOU MAY BE ABLE TO REMOVE THEIR TEETH AND REDUCE THE RISK OF A BITE, BUT IN GENERAL NOTHING POSITIVE COMES FROM TRYING TO CLIMB ONTO A ZOMBIE AND RIDING OFF INTO THE SUNSET.

WORKING WITH THE DEAD

There are five key principles that all survivors should be aware of when working with zombies.

1 SNACK RADIUS

The first rule of working with the dead is that zombies will always reach, grab and bite for the flesh of the living. Creatures may have been de-toothed and de-clawed but you should always be aware of a zombie's 'snack radius' – the range at which it can grab a human – and manage your own safety carefully. It doesn't need to be a bite that kills as an infected scratch can do just as much harm.

2 SAFE STORAGE

Zombies must be safely stored any time they are not in use. Basic requirements include a sealed cage, preferably with a door that opens inwards. Any cage should be well maintained and bars are discouraged as the dead can easily reach through and grab one of the living. Storage areas should be well-lit, well-ventilated and, where possible, kept at a cool temperature.

3 COLLECTION TECHNIQUES

Always use approved techniques to restrain a zombie. An extended and locking neck-brace on the end of a pole is the best method. Such operations should never be attempted alone and it is recommended that each zombie is captured and then stored safely before efforts commence to secure another creature.

4 ZOMBIE BEHAVIOR

Over several weeks in confinement, a zombie may appear to become 'dormant', particularly if it has little or no close contact with living humans. Be aware that a ghoul can snap out of this dormant state in seconds, becoming as dangerous as when it was first caught. Always 'wake' a zombie that appears to be in this state – normally, any noise or odor of the living will achieve this.

5 OTHER DISEASES

Cleanliness and personal hygiene cannot be over-emphasized when working with and handling the dead. Zombies are a veritable greenhouse for bacteria and infection, some of which are as dangerous as the zombie virus itself. Always wash and disinfect yourself after any contact with the dead and use protective clothing and eye wear at all times.

THE ZOMBIE CLEARING SYSTEM (ZCS)

The ZCS is a coordinated strategy for clearing an area, typically urban, which is infested with zombies. It was developed by the Ministry of Zombies in 2008, building on the new advances in zombiology and the experience of hundreds of zombie fighters. It is a system that can be used over and over again to transform a wasteland dominated by the dead into an area where frightened survivors can start to rebuild. Remember, not every battle in the zombie war will be a desperate last stand or a mass-zombie killing raid – you also need to think about gathering together survivors and developing your settlement into something that can support the real war against the dead.

HOW IT WORKS

The underlying principle of the ZCS is to isolate a substantial area, for example, several city blocks, by building a reasonable perimeter around the whole site. Your whole team will be involved in this task and should make use of any natural barriers such as rivers. You can also blow up buildings to block roads or seal houses to form a makeshift 'wall'. To complete the next phase of the system, divide your teams into three, each with their own roles: the Kill Squad to clear the sealed off area of the dead, the Clearing Squad to deal with any remaining ghouls, and the Rebuild Squad to make the environment habitable for survivors.

TEAM 1
THE KILL SQUAD KS
CLUBBING THE ZOMBIES ONE AT A TIME

Gung-ho zombie killers operating in squads of 4–5 fighters, these teams are sent in once an area has been sealed off. Generally, the squads work together for a general sweep of the main areas then split up for the nerve-wracking business of house-to-house zombie clearance. After clearing a building, they chalk or paint a large 'KS' on the door to show that it's been cleared. Kill Squad members must be tough, strong and experienced in zombie combat. They often see themselves as the elite of the zombie clearing system and you should develop cool team identities to help reinforce this.

TEAM 2
THE CLEARING SQUAD [CS]
FIGHTING THE DEAD WITH RUBBER GLOVES

Working in the Clearing Squad is no job for the faint-hearted. It's these survivors who clear the bodies from the streets and re-enter 'KS' buildings to clean up any blood splatter or remains. Once they've cleared a building, they add a 'CS' to the door to show it's been cleared for the next stage. Clearing Squad members must be able to handle themselves in combat as they will run into the odd zombie missed by the first sweep, but they also need a constitution of iron and the cleaning skills to match.

TEAM 3
THE REBUILD SQUAD [RS]
NAILING GHOULS TO THE FLOOR WITH DIY

The smallest team in terms of numbers, the Rebuild Squad follows on from the Clearing Squad and is responsible for ensuring that buildings are once again habitable for humans. They repair doors and generally zombie-proof the lower levels, turning each repaired home into a mini-bastion. They open up chimneys to create fire places and complete any insulation work required for a winter without heating. Once a building is fit for habitation, the squad adds an 'RS' to the door and may even add an 'H' if the dwelling is particularly habitable. Squad members are typically carpenters, plumbers and engineers.

SURVIVOR GROUPS

Z-Day will change everything. The pillars of society will collapse along with any forces of central government, law and order. It is important to remember that as you develop your survivor community and start to take the war to the zombies, you will come into increasing contact with other survivor groups. Many will be 'normal' bands of survivors, only too willing to join your fight. Others will be far more dangerous.

As your scouts and foragers move further afield from your main settlement, you must ensure they have clear instructions on how to deal with the various groups and individuals they are likely to encounter. Be clear with them that the zombies are not the only threat out there.

A First-Contact Protocol has already been outlined for dealing with minor survivor groups and how to bring them into your community. Group First-Contact Protocols are more in-depth and include a range of responses based on the group you encounter.

Your teams should study the profiles of the groups and individuals they are likely to meet. There are several types of group that should be avoided at all costs unless you have the resources to engage in full conflict with them.

THE CITWR PROFILE

Using a team of post-apocalyptic experts from across the world, the Ministry of Zombies has developed the CITWR system to help your teams recognise and manage the most common groups of the wasteland.

CAPABILITY   The strength of the group, its numbers, set-up, resource level and military capability.

INTENT   The level of hostile intent towards either your community or activities in the zombie war.

THREAT LEVEL   The likelihood that this group will act with malcontent towards your community or the war effort.

WEAPONS   A measure of how dangerous and skilful the group is in terms of its firearms and other weapons such as blades and booby traps.

RESPONSE   Guidelines on how your forces should manage such a group and advice on any protocols for first contact.

SURVIVING THE APOCALYPSE
PROFILE OF SURVIVORS

A Psychological Profile of Survivors after Day 120. This information was calculated using the FBI's complex modelling profiling system.

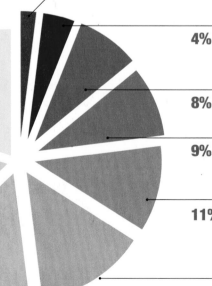

20% STILL HIDING
'Scared, so very scared!'

17% FIGHTING THE ZOMBIE WAR
'I'll die fighting for humanity if I have to!'

15% ORDINARY SURVIVORS
'A bit of foraging, a bit of hiding, always scared.'

2% DOING SICK THINGS
'I do bad things and I love it!'

4% PRETENDING TO BE ZOMBIES
'They accept me now.'

8% LONELY DRIFTERS
'I'm safer on my own.'

9% DYSTOPIAN KNOW-IT-ALL'S
'I TOLD YOU SO!'

11% CRAZY WASTELAND WARRIORS
'I ate cat yesterday. Tastes better than squirrel.'

14% LOVIN' IT
'I hated the old life anyway.'

MINISTRY OF ZOMBIES

SCAVENGERS OR LOOTERS

Numerous in the early months, some will take advantage of the end of the world to riot and grab what they can. Lacking the culture and infrastructure of an organised gang, some looters and petty thieves will join together as opportunistic and often violent looters – scouring the ruins for any survivors who can't defend themselves.

'GIVE ME ALL YOUR SUPPLIES OR I'M GONNA POP A CAP IN YOUR ASS!'

CAPABILITY

Most looters and thieves will be eaten or killed within the first month of the crisis. Opportunistic and ill-prepared, many will be caught in the open stealing items such as TVs and laptops – goods useful to them. However, a few will band together in groups of up to 30. They will work together to 'do over' survivor houses and look to survive themselves through looting and theft.

INTENT

Survival is their number-one priority. They will not want to see any return to law and order and will resist it but lack the capability for any sustained conflict. You may even find them offering to 'sell' your settlement their ill-gotten gains. Be aware, this won't just be foraged goods, this will be supplies taken from other survivors!

THREAT LEVEL

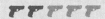

Thieves and looters are reluctant to engage in outright conflict with another organised group. Their profile is to pick on weaker targets. However, they can be dangerous when cornered and will be armed.

WEAPONS

Handguns held sideways are the weapon of choice for most urban groups whilst rogue grandma will be armed with anything from a 19th-century musket to a pump-action shotgun.

RESPONSE

You must be firm with this group. Defend your own territory with force and make plain your warnings about their activities. They can be a useful source for supplies, but over the long term thieves and looters must be dealt with. Some group members will willingly join you in the zombie war.

FAMILY SURVIVAL GROUPS

By far the most common organised groups, these will be hungry and desperate bands of 'normal' survivors eking out a living in the wasteland and just about holding it together.

'JUST TURN AROUND AND KEEP WALKING.'
'WE DON'T NEED NO HELP!'
'CAN WE JOIN YOU?'

CAPABILITY

This groups tend to be small, mostly fewer than 12, and based around an extended family. They may have added additional neighbours to the group over the months of struggle. Resource-wise they will be just hanging on and typically armed with a few firearms and hand weapons. The rural farming variant of this group will be hardier and more independent as they have a more secure food source.

INTENT

Like many in the wasteland, family survival groups just want to stay alive. They most likely have children or the elderly in their home base and are desperately trying to carry on despite the ravenous dead just outside their window. There will be very little hostility towards your patrols unless they think you are looters.

THREAT LEVEL

The only time one of these groups will attack is when they consider you an immediate threat. They will have been attacked before and may be over-anxious in opening fire at any strangers.

WEAPONS

They may be armed with a few guns, but they will be ruthless in defense of their family. Grandad may be a Vietnam veteran and is likely to opt for the dwarf axe he bought on the internet.

RESPONSE

You must communicate your intentions towards this group clearly. Once they realise you are an organised community, fighting back against the dead, most will happily join up. Some will take longer so be patient. Also be aware that these groups can bring numbers of dependents into your settlement.

SURVIVING THE APOCALYPSE

▷ INNER-CITY GANGS

These tightly organized criminal gangs dominate many urban locations across the world and the zombie apocalypse, or 'zompoc', will be the perfect opportunity for them to increase their 'hood'.

'THIS IS OUR HOOD SO GET OUT OF THE HOUSE.'

**'THAT'S NOT VERY FRIENDLY,
WE ONLY WANNA SHARE!'**

CAPABILITY
Well-organized and bound together by strong oaths of family, loyalty and upbringing, these groups will be a powerful force long after other criminals have disappeared under a wave of zombies. Numbers can be anything up to 100 core members but expect them to recruit big time when the dead rise.

INTENT
After years struggling against society and the police, this will be the time for gangs to take what they want. Expansion will be on the agenda, as will defeating any close rival gangs.

THREAT LEVEL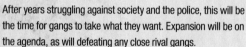
Medium to High. Inner-city gangs will be well-armed and motivated. They could be powerful allies or deadly opponents. Where their agenda revolves around drugs and human trafficking, you will have little option but to fight against them.

WEAPONS
Many of these gangs were 'tooled up' before the zompoc and with ready access to firearms, you can expect them to be heavily armed by the time you encounter them. They may not be formally trained, but they will be equally deadly with hand weapons such as baseball bats.

RESPONSE
Always learn about a street gang before opening up an attack. Treat them with respect and find out what their agenda is. Many will be young people thrown together for survival in a location that was deadly enough before the zombies arrived. If you can talk them round they could prove to be very useful fighters.

▷ BARONS OF THE ZOMPOC

Powerful individuals who have taken full advantage of the end of civilization to build their own feudal kingdoms. Sometimes a particularly powerful gang leader, politician or business executive, even a bank manager, can evolve into this fully post-apocalyptic role.

'JOIN US AND END THIS PATHETIC ZOMBIE WAR.'

'I COULD USE A FIGHTER LIKE YOU.'

CAPABILITY
Barons are well-armed and equipped, with a fortified base and a close cohort of henchmen and women. They rule their local area, taking what they want from any survivors and even enslaving them as serfs. Some organized crime groups have all the infrastructure to move into this category.

INTENT
Power is everything to a Baron of the Zompoc. They are ambitious individuals with one paranoid eye on preserving what they have and the other on expansion and growing their 'kingdom'.

THREAT LEVEL
High. Barons will see any rival power as a threat to their cruel reign of terror. They could be powerful allies in your fight against the zombies but are likely to be distrustful allies. Their agenda is self-serving in their quest for more power.

WEAPONS
This group typically has stocks of firearms from before the zompoc to support their criminal activities. They'll have the access and knowledge to use them. Favorite weapons include the handgun, flick knife and knuckle duster.

RESPONSE
It may be possible to reach an uneasy peace with a Baron, for example by agreeing to 'spheres of influence'. However, this will not last. Do not allow this group to infiltrate your settlement and in any direct conflict, go for the Baron and his or her loyal cadre. Take out these individuals and the clan will fall.

DOOMSDAY FANATICS

The end of the world will see the emergence of a whole spectrum of cults and doomsday groups. Many will be dedicated to fighting the zombie menace, and these groups can easily integrate into your operation. However, others will have a more sinister and downright evil agenda.

'HOW DO I KNOW THE END IS NEAR? THE UNIVERSE TOLD ME.'

CAPABILITY

Cults are typically centred around one charismatic leader. Expect numbers to be anything from a small group up to 30 or 40. They will be totally dedicated, often sporting a vacant look and talking about 'the way'.

INTENT

This will vary from bringing about the end of mankind to growing a group for the self-interested if not self-appointed leader. Any interference with their group will lead to serious conflict. In some battles, their fighters will be fanatical, only stopped by death.

THREAT LEVEL

Medium. Approach these groups with caution. Carefully assess them and do not leap to conclusions based on their 'friendly' introduction. Learn about their cult beliefs and assess their weapons capability – some will be extremely well-armed.

WEAPONS

Many twisted post-apocalyptic cults will have the 'harvesting of the living' on the agenda and so a traditional scythe will be their favored weapon. Expect the most organized cults to be well-equipped with other weapons and firearms.

RESPONSE
Always treat religious communities with respect, but where they are obvious cults, be tactful and cautious. Do not go to war without good reason and target the leader if possible.

CANNIBALS

With food scarce, some survivor groups will descend into cannibalism. Generally, this is a one-way street and once they have a taste for human flesh, they will rapidly descend into a group that regularly preys on other survivors.

'ONCE YOU'VE TRIED IT, YOU'LL NEVER GO BACK.'

'YOU LOOK SO HEALTHY AND WELL. DO YOU HAVE MANY FAT PEOPLE AT YOUR CAMP?'

CAPABILITY

These groups tend to be small, extended family operations in which members are closely bound together in their debauched lifestyles. All social norms will have broken down once the cannibalism taboo is shattered.

INTENT

Cannibal groups have no ambitions to take over. Their battle is to secure sources of human flesh. With this in mind, you will rarely come into conflict with them unless they are taking your people.

THREAT LEVEL

Low to Medium. The main impact of allowing a cannibal group to continue unhindered will be on the morale of the settlement. Knowing that the zombies are out there waiting is bad enough without the addition of devious humans as well. Cannibal groups cannot be allowed to survive in the medium term and fighting them will often mean wiping them out.

WEAPONS

The weapon of choice for cannibals will be the trusty meat cleaver. Sharp and with enough power to take an arm off in one swipe. Don't get too close.

RESPONSE
Groups will not declare themselves as cannibals on first contact. Ensure your teams can spot the warning signs such as human bones scattered around within their complex and any human adornments they may be wearing. Be prepared to use force as these fanatics will not be able to integrate back into 'normal' society.

SURVIVING THE APOCALYPSE

▷ EX-MILITARY AND ROBOCOPS

There is no question that our armed forces will put up a fight after the dead rise, but the sheer number of walking corpses will doom them to defeat. With this disintegration of command and control, various armed units will be left, without orders. Many will organize, using their experience in the forces to create a new group.

'I AM THE LAW! RESPECT MY AUTHORITY.'

'I AM REQUISITIONING YOUR SUPPLIES!'

CAPABILITY
These groups tend to have a hierarchical structure, with a former leader allocated the role of 'Commander'. Numbering anything from a small patrol to a battalion, these well-armed and trained groups will be in a strong position to survive as society collapses.

INTENT
The intention of this survivor group varies wildly from wanting to bring all of those left alive under their 'safe' control to being especially eager to link with other organized groups. Basically, in the wrong hands, an ex-military group will become little better than a strict robber baron with an authoritarian tilt. They can be brutal, decisive and quick to act.

THREAT LEVEL
High. Any encounter with a member of this group will be potentially risky. They must therefore be considered highly dangerous and any contact must be tightly managed. Over time, more groups will be become dominated by power-hungry leaders so after a few months, most will be hostile.

WEAPONS
These forces will be well-equipped with military- and police-grade firearms and supplies. One of the few groups with heavy weapons and even armored vehicles.

RESPONSE
One tactic to attempt with ex-military groups is to recast your group as the 'central command'. You in effect will take over as their commander. Depending on their current leader, this can be a risky strategy. Open conflict with this group is not recommended, but they can prove to be invaluable allies in the war against the walking dead.

▷ MUTANTS OF THE WASTELAND

The zombie virus is always mutating and adding the possibility of a nuclear strike to clear cities of the dead. Survivors could encounter any number of genetic and zombic mutations.

'I AM THE NEW INHERITOR OF THE WORLD.'

'SOMEONE PLEASE JUST KILL ME!'

'DID I SEE YOUR FIGHTER. NO, I DON'T THINK I DID.'

CAPABILITY
Mutations are likely to be one-offs. They may be dangerous in combat, particularly if they are human/zombie hybrids, with the ability to think but with all the trappings of the ghoul. Most will be sad specimens doomed to wander the wastelands scavenging for food.

INTENT
Survival is their aim. Most will cower in the shadows, keeping well away from your patrols. You may occasionally lose a fighter where they have been snatched for food, but on the whole, mutants will have no great designs on your settlement if they are left alone.

THREAT LEVEL
Low. They can be dangerous in unarmed combat and there is the threat that they could spread a mutated form of the zombie virus. Avoid any bites or stings from mutants.

WEAPONS
Mutants could have a whole arsenal of unnatural weaponry from poison stingers in their tail to sharp bong hooks on their tentacles. They won't normally use firearms.

RESPONSE
Do not actively search out this group. Where mutants become an issue, you may need to 'cleanse' the situation, but for the most part, as long as they are not too powerful, give them a wide berth and leave them in peace.

WALKING-DEAD LOVED ONES (WDL)

Sick individuals who keep family members or other zombies at home.

'THERE MIGHT BE A CURE OUT THERE.'

'MY MOTHER IS STILL IN THERE SOMEWHERE.'

CAPABILITY

More often than not, WDLs work alone so the only challenge will be if you are trying to break into their dwelling. They have very little offensive capability. They will have weapons they started with and possibly a few more which have been foraged. Generally, they won't leave the side of their 'loved ones'.

INTENT

All WDLs want is to be with the one they love. They have no intentions towards your group unless you try to take out the ghouls in their care.

THREAT LEVEL

Very low. This group will not bother your settlement as long as you do not disturb them. There is the additional side benefit that they will take out the odd zombie that catches their eye.

WEAPONS

Weapons for self-defense only. Grandad's old shotgun is most common. Another favorite is the sledge hammer. This group is also a fan of booby traps so if your forces storm their house, be wary of some deadly traps.

RESPONSE

Your scouts may make first contact with this group, but it is prudent to keep your distance. If they offer to introduce you to the rest of their 'family', politely refuse.

AMAZONS OF THE APOCALYPSE

In the carnage and chaos of the first few months, people will band together for mutual protection. Some women will see this as an opportunity to break free of the discrimination in society. Using their growing skills in the martial arts, you may see the emergence of groups of amazons of the wasteland.

'OMG, ANTI-ZOMBIE BFFS FOREVER.'

CAPABILITY

Fiercely loyal to one another and tightly bound together in a 'sisterhood of survival', these women will be skilful fighters and may verge on Baron-of-Zompoc-like behavior.

INTENT

This group will rarely be hostile for no reason. If they attack then it is likely that one of your patrols strayed into their 'territory'. The primary aim of this group is survival and possibly to liberate others suffering under, say, a local Baron of the Zompoc.

THREAT LEVEL

Medium. This group may have been drawn together for protection, but their offensive skills are very real. If you cross them, they will respond with fury and force. They have all the skills to be a deadly opponent.

WEAPONS

Archery clubs report over 51,000 new female members across America in 2012 so the weapon of choice will be the bow, backed up by firearms. Martial arts clubs added a further 110,000 new female participants in combat.

RESPONSE

Always send a female fighter as your first contact and approach them unarmed and with clear intentions. An Amazon group will never merge with your own immediately but you can build up a strong working partnership against the dead in battle.

SURVIVING THE APOCALYPSE

⊳ END-OF-THE-WORLD SCIENTISTS

With an ongoing mission to either kill mankind or cure the zombie virus, these isolated and lonely survivors could be either a curse or an invaluable ally in your battle with the dead.

'I JUST NEED MORE BODIES TO EXPERIMENT ON.'

'SOON ALL WILL KNOW MY NAME!'

'DO YOU HAVE ANY SPIDERMAN COMICS?'

CAPABILITY

Tending to work in total isolation, scientists working on the virus will be sealed away from the carnage in high-tech domes of safety. They may have one hard-pressed assistant, but other than that, they will be the sole survivors at their site. Their military capability is almost all defensive and may include automated defenses such as turret machine guns.

INTENT

Most end-of-the-world types want to be left alone. Even if they are working to develop an airborne strain of the zombie virus, they will not be interested in minor groups of survivors. They have bigger things on their mind. If they are working on a cure, invariably nothing will be ready for testing.

THREAT LEVEL

Low. These research projects rarely come to anything. If left undisturbed, this group will happily work away in isolation. Even if they run out of supplies, they will not venture out, often preferring to take their own lives than face the dead.

WEAPONS

It's all about defense for this group. They will be safely sealed inside, defended by bulletproof glass and thick steel doors. The complex may be protected by automated defenses.

RESPONSE

You won't find this group unless you go looking for it. The effort required to get into their 'lair' is often not worth it, with end-of-the-world scientists offering little more than vacant threats or promised deliverance. Best practice is to leave them alone.

⊳ GENERATION Z

Very few family units will survive the zombie apocalypse intact and where children become orphaned or separated, they will herd together into gangs of youths known to zombie psychologists as Generation Z.

'OMG! I AM SO GONNA SKIN YOU ALIVE!'

'YOU WERE LIKE ON OUR PATCH LIKE. THERE'S NO WAY YOU CAN GET AWAY WITH IT. LIKE.'

CAPABILITY

These groups will tend to be up around 40 in size. Any larger and they tend to splinter. Based around teenagers, kids of various ages will group together, bound by a fierce sense of loyalty. Without any parental guidance or authority, they will be capable of great kindness and cruelty. They will be very able to defend themselves.

INTENT

Like many groups, survival is the name of the game. Depending on the leadership they may be aggressive towards outsiders and will have little interest in your zombie war from the start.

THREAT LEVEL

Low to Medium. The main flashpoint with Generation Z will be around foraging and supplies. If you don't enter their territory, you will be unlikely to come into direct contact with them. However, some of the children will grow up after Z-day, and this world will be all they've ever known. They will be tough, seasoned zombie fighters, more than capable of killing to survive.

WEAPONS

These kids will be experts in the use of the catapult for hunting and, make no mistake, it can also be a deadly weapon against human opponents. They are also likely to be skilled in firearms, copying the handgun held sideways stance of larger gangs.

RESPONSE

These feral children can be unpredictable and violent so a cautious and soft approach is required. Do not come across as the 'adult' or too heavy handed. Respect their boundaries and earn their appreciation. It will be a long and fraught process to bring Generation Z children into your settlement.

 MINISTRY OF ZOMBIES

MAD LONERS

For some, the madness of the zombie apocalypse will be too much. Many mad loner and crazed survivors will have started out within a group, perhaps it was overrun and massacred. Now, their only agenda is chaos and ever-increasing levels of craziness.

'I'M NEVER ALONE WITH MY INVISIBLE FRIENDS.'

'THE VOICES KEEP SPEAKING TO ME. THEY ARE TELLING ME TO LIGHT FIRES!'

CAPABILITY

One individual can do a lot of damage and you can expect these individual activities to range from running around naked dodging the zombies to lighting fires and screaming that they are going to 'burn everything away'. This profile always operates alone.

INTENT

The response of these individuals to outsiders varies greatly. Many will simply hide and come out only when you are gone. Others will sneakily follow your patrols back to base and then spy on your activities. Most will just want to be left alone.

THREAT LEVEL

Medium. The level of insanity with these individuals ranges from slightly crazed to homicidal maniac. The most dangerous individuals may embark on a killing spree or attack your patrols, but the most likely threat is their habit of starting fires. If one of these uncontrolled blazes reaches your survival settlement, things could get very ugly, very quickly.

WEAPONS

Fire is the mad loner's best friend and greatest weapon. They will be armed with other firearms and weapons, but they have a habit of starting blazes with cans of gasoline where they can do most damage.

RESPONSE

If you have an experienced counsellor, you may be able to talk these characters around, but it is unlikely. The particularly violent ones can do a significant amount of damage in which case decisive action will be required.

WASTELAND WARRIORS

For some men and women, the death and carnage of the zombie apocalypse will be an awful liberation. The pillars and constraints of society will be gone and they wander the ruins of civilizations looking tough and offering rock-hard one liners.

'I USED TO WORK IN A CALL CENTER.'

'I DON'T WANT ANY TROUBLE, I'M JUST LOOKING FOR MY SON.'

CAPABILITY

Warriors of the wasteland typically survive alone. Sometimes there are two but never more than this. They will be carrying what they need to survive, living day-by-day and foraging where they can. They will be well-armed and skilled with their weapons. At the start there may be many of these types, but only the best will survive as the months progress.

INTENT

Generally, warriors are good guys or girls. They are often driven on by the loss of their family or maybe even in search of them. Their old lives are in ruins and the zompoc has transformed them. They are well-adapted to survive in zombie-infested areas.

THREAT LEVEL

Low. This group will rarely threaten your survivor community unless they are attacked first. Also, do not try to restrict these individuals from travelling through your 'territory'. They are usually loners and will only forage what they need.

WEAPONS

Warriors of the wasteland will have every type of weapon in that backpack, from shotgun to handgun, machete to samurai sword.

RESPONSE

Be firm but friendly towards these warriors. They could be powerful allies in the war against the zombies. Respect their freedom to roam and offer them smaller missions for payment to help bring them into your fold. Offering to replenish their supplies and ammunition will be well-received and help you to build a relationship.

GLOSSARY

apocalypse A great disaster; a sudden and very bad event that causes much fear, loss, or destruction.

barricade (v) To block (something) so that people or things cannot enter or leave; (n) a temporary wall, fence, or similar structure that is built to prevent people from entering a place or area.

cannibal A person who eats the flesh of human beings or an animal that eats its own kind.

corpse A dead body.

decomposition The process by which dead organic matter separates into simpler substances; decay; rot.

desiccated Dried up; drained of emotional or intellectual vitality.

gastric Of, relating to, or near the stomach.

ghoul An evil creature in frightening stories that robs graves and eats dead bodies.

metamorphosis A major change in the appearance or character of someone or something ; a major change in the form or structure of some animals or insects that happens as the animal or insect becomes an adult.

mutation A significant and basic alteration; change; a relatively permanent change in hereditary material.

outbreak A sudden start or increase of fighting or disease.

perimeter The outside edge of an area or surface; a line or strip bounding or protecting an area.

plague A large number of harmful or annoying things ; a disease that causes death and that spreads quickly to a large number of people.

post-apocalyptic The period of time and disastrous conditions that follow after an apocalypse; the aftermath of a massive and highly destructive disaster.

quarantine The period of time during which a person or animal that has a disease or that might have a disease is kept away from others to prevent the disease from spreading ; the situation of being kept away from others to prevent a disease from spreading.

siege A situation in which soldiers or police officers surround a city, building, etc., in order to try to take control of it ; a serious and lasting attack of something.

survivalist A person who believes that government and society will soon fail completely and who stores food, weapons, etc., in order to be prepared to survive when that happens.

symptom A change in the body or mind which indicates that a disease is present ; a change which shows that something bad exists : a sign of something bad.

transmission The act or process by which something, such as a virus, is spread or passed from one person or thing to another.

undead A creature that has movement, volition, and will, but is not technically alive, such as a zombie or vampire, and must feed upon the living in order to continue its existence.

virus The causative agent of an infectious disease; any of a large group of submicroscopic infective agents that are regarded either as extremely simple microorganisms or as extremely complex molecules that are capable of growth and multiplication only in living cells, and that cause various important diseases in humans, lower animals, or plants.

vulnerable Easily hurt or harmed physically, mentally, or emotionally ; open to attack, harm, or damage.

FOR MORE INFORMATION

Center for Disease Control and Prevention's Zombie Preparedness Web Page
1600 Clifton Road
Atlanta, GA 30329-4027
Phone: 800-CDC-INFO (800-232-4636)
Website: http://www.cdc.gov/phpr/zombies.htm
http://blogs.cdc.gov/publichealthmatters/2011/05/preparedness-101-zombie-apocalypse/
What first began as a tongue in cheek campaign by the Center for Disease Control and Prevention to engage new audiences with preparedness messages has proven to be a very effective platform. It continues to reach and engage a wide variety of audiences on all hazards preparedness via Zombie Preparedness.

The Folklore Society,
c/o The Warburg Institute
Woburn Square
London WC1H 0AB, UK
Phone: +44 (0) 207 862 8564
Website: http://folklore-society.com
The Folklore Society (FLS) is a scholarly society devoted to the study of traditional culture in all its forms. It was founded in London in 1878 and was one of the first organizations established in the world for the study of folklore. The Folklore Society's interest and expertise covers such topics as traditional music, song, dance and drama, narrative, arts and crafts, customs, and belief. It is also interested in popular religion, traditional and regional food, folk medicine, children's folklore, traditional sayings, proverbs, rhymes, and jingles. Its aims are to foster the research and documentation of folklore worldwide, and to make the results of such study available to all, whether members of the Society or not.

Zombie Research Society (ZRS)
Contact: Mogk@ZRS.me
Website: http://zombieresearchsociety.com
Zombie Research Society (ZRS) was founded in 2007 as an organization dedicated to the historic, cultural, and scientific study of the living dead. The organization has grown to include hundreds of thousands of active members across the world. Its team of experts currently consists of a number of prominent authors, artists, and academics committed to the real-life research of zombies and the undead, as well as a core group of volunteers who handle the daily management of ZRS.

Zombie Squad, Inc.
P.O. Box 63124
St. Louis, MO 63163-3124
Email: chapters@zombiehunters.org
Phone: (888) 495-4052
Website: https://www.zombiehunters.org
Zombie Squad is the world's pre-eminent non-stationary cadaver suppression task force, committed to helping defend your neighborhood and town from the hordes of the undead. It provides trained and motivated highly-skilled zombie suppression professionals as well as zombie survival consultants.

Web sites

Due to the changing nature of Internet links, Rosen Publishing has developed an online list of Web sites related to the subject of this book. This site is updated regularly. Please use this link to access this list:

http://www.rosenlinks.com/SZW/Prep

FOR FURTHER READING

Austin, John. So Now You're a Zombie: A Handbook for the Newly Undead. Chicago, IL: Chicago Review Press, 2010.

Borgenicht, David, and Ben H. Winters. The Worst-Case Scenario Survival Handbook: Paranormal. San Francisco, CA: Chronicle Books, 2011.

Brooks, Max. World War Z: An Oral History of the Zombie War. New York, NY: Three Rivers Press, 2007.

Brooks, Max. The Zombie Survival Guide: Complete Protection from the Living Dead. New York, NY: Broadway Books, 2003.

Emerson, Clint. 100 Deadly Skills: The SEAL Operative's Guide to Eluding Pursuers, Evading Capture, and Surviving Any Dangerous Situation. New York, NY: Touchstone, 2015.

Lonely Planet. How to Survive Anything: A Visual Guide to Laughing in the Face of Adversity. Oakland, CA: Lonely Planet, 2015.

Luckhurst, Roger. Zombies: A Cultural History. London, England: Reaktion, Books, 2015.

Ma, Roger. The Zombie Combat Manual: A Guide to Fighting the Living Dead. New York, NY: Berkley, 2010.

MacWelch, Tim, and the editors of Outdoor Life. How to Survive Anything: From Animal Attacks to the End of the World (and Everything in Between). San Francisco, CA: Weldon Owen, 2015.

MacWelch, Tim, and the editors of Outdoor Life. Prepare for Anything Survival Manual: 338 Essential Skills. San Francisco, CA: Weldon Owen, 2014.

Mogk, Matt. Everything You Ever Wanted to Know About Zombies. New York, NY: Gallery Books, 2011.

Piven, Joshua, and David Borgenicht. The Complete Worst-Case Scenario Survival Handbook. San Francisco, CA: Chronicle Books, 2007.

Piven, Joshua, and David Borgenicht. The Worst-Case Scenario Survival Handbook: Extreme Edition. San Francisco, CA: Chronicle Books, 2005.

Rawles, James Wesley. How to Survive the End of the World as We Know It: Tactics, Techniques, and Technologies for Uncertain Times. New York, NY: Penguin Books, 2009.

Wilson, Lauren, and Kristian Bauthus. The Art of Eating Through the Zombie Apocalypse: A Cookbook and Culinary Survival Guide. Dallas, TX: Smart Pop, 2014.

Wiseman, John "Lofty." SAS Survival Handbook: The Ultimate Guide to Surviving Anywhere. New York, NY: William Morrow, 2014.

AUTHOR'S ACKNOWLEDGMENTS

I hope you enjoy reading this book as much as we all did writing, designing and illustrating it. When we started, there were unbelievers working on the team, now we are all ready for the zombie apocalypse and slightly more paranoid than before. I want to thank my partners in crime Louise and Richard at Haynes for all their hard work and patience – both were last seen heading for their secure locations in Scotland. Also, to my wife for her tireless support as we spent weekends testing everything from crossbows to living in a sealed concrete bunker – see my website for details and more insanity – www.ministryofzombies.com. Finally, I want to mention all my family back in Ashford. I come from a close family – not in a weird or banjo-playing way – we just get along and this book is dedicated to them and my home-town.

⚠ WARNING!